DOG DAD

DOG DAD

How Animals Bring Out The Best In Us
And Can Help Save The World

TOPHER BROPHY

VERTEL
PUBLISHING

Dog Dad

© 2022 by Topher Brophy

For information, contact Vertel Publishing at
2837 Rivers Avenue
Charleston, South Carolina 29405

First edition

Manufactured in the United States of America
1 3 5 7 9 10 8 6 4 2

Hardback ISBN: 978-1-64112-034-0
eBook ISBN: 978-1-64112-035-7

Library of Congress Cataloging-in-Publication Data has been applied for.

To Rosenberg:

Your unconditional love allowed me to love myself, which changed the course of my life. While there will always be so many things that will drive me to tears, knowing there are beings as pure as you will always make life more tolerable. I will cherish every hair on your fluffy head while you are here and every second of our beautiful memories until I breathe my last breath.

Thank you for being my love battery, my son, my teacher, my best friend, and my soul mate. I love you more than words and am eternally lucky you exist.

With a happy heart,
Your proud dad

Contents

Chapter 1

Introduction

FELLOW *HOMO SAPIENS*, **WHAT TRIGGERED** your interest in this book? Maybe the cover caught your eye or you're familiar with me from social media, a TV screen, or the news. Perhaps you found the title intriguing, or maybe someone simply recommended you read it.

Whatever the reason, I'm intoxicated you're here.

And now that you have gotten past the first two paragraphs, I'm certain I know two things about you. First, you are a principled person who loves animals, and second, and more specifically, you have a soft spot for our species' closest, most compatible friends—*Canis lupus familiaris.*

So does the fact that you hold in your hands a book written by a guy known for dressing like his dog and vacillating between being candidly emotive and brazenly ludicrous mean you are in for some fluffy and disposable schlock? Or will this be yet another sappy, saccharine, predictable self-help story? The answer to both questions is a resounding no.

I wrote this book because I was compelled to relate both my most vivid catastrophes and my most inconceivable triumphs because, like all humans, I have suffered, and I feel a responsibility to share what I have learned.

For the majority of my life, I found it painful to be a human. I hated myself and held human nature to be cruel, cosmetic, and morally corrupt. I constantly judged others, wore a permanent scowl, and had zero ability to make emotional connections or sustain friendships. This pain came on early in my life, increasing gradually, then crescendoing, until it became so intolerable I was very nearly ready to bring things to an end. I had no idea it was possible to live *without* incessant pain.

Then, at precisely that point, when life could not possibly get any worse, an angel entered my life and changed everything. This being became my identity decoder, my self-esteem booster, my social connector, mentor, teacher, muse, and best friend—the catalyst for a change so monumental that at times you may question if this is a work of wildly inventive fiction. It is not; every word is true.

This canine angel enabled me to discover my passion, identify my life's mission, find my life partner, start a family, understand that inherent good exists in everyone, and have certainty that the world, despite its challenges, is an enchantingly awe-inspiring place. Although it is still hard for me to comprehend, I am now the person I've always dreamed of becoming: a person able to handle life's inevitable ups and downs, a person who strives to speak for the silent, who champions optimism and thoughtfulness, who fights to make the world a better place.

Yes, some of the occurrences I write about are uncanny, but that's just part of our precarious condition. And unfathomably alchemical energies have a way of treating that condition, of teaching us how to better ride the wave of being alive, and, if we let them, of maximizing our happiness. What unleashed those energies in my case was the caring love of an animal.

So in this book, I will prove the truth of its subtitle—that animals can make us better people and help save the world. Given the proliferating plethora of problems we all face in the world and within ourselves, I feel certain you'll agree we desperately need to realize both aims, now more than ever. And for those of you who, like me, have felt insecure or out of place, been ridiculed or called "weird," or had a hard time getting through life or dealing with the occasional cruelty of the world, this book presents one miraculous solution.

As you read the story of how my animal son, my best friend, my teacher, and my love battery helped me, I hope you will see how becoming an animal parent and learning from your animal child can have a miraculous impact on your life. And if enough of us experience enough such impacts, we really can save the world.

Chapter 2

Everyone Dies

MEMORIES ARE FINICKY AND AT times unforgiving. We can recall the big arcs of our lives, but specifics are either etched into our minds—and we carry their sounds and smells forever—or they go poof and evaporate, as if they never happened. What sticks may seem like a mystery, but I believe there is always a reason for why we remember some details over others, as the sum of our memories creates the pathologies that make us who we come to be, flaws and all.

I grew up in New York City in the late 1980s in an incredibly decent, hardworking, and morally minded family, with fair, responsible, and unbelievably loving parents. They worked long hours, and we lived comfortable middle-class lives. And as open-minded baby boomers with hippie history, they exposed me, above all other priorities, to the melting pot of diversity the city had to offer. We lived downtown on a busy four-lane street, where the pedestrian traffic included everyone from a family like us to patients of a methadone clinic and residents of a local homeless shelter, one of whom seared himself into my mind in a memory that came to define my early childhood.

I was six years old, walking hand in hand with my mother on a late-spring Saturday under a clear sky full of pollen that tickled my nose with allergies. We were a block and a half from our apartment, on our way to Goldfarb's, a family-owned stationery store that smartly stocked Matchbox cars, which I collected. This route meant we had to walk past a homeless man standing beside the glass doors to McDonald's, out of which leaked the scent of processed deliciousness.

As we passed, he and I locked eyes and, for an instant, became transfixed with each other. His eyes were cloudy but still piercingly aqua, and his clothing was a mixture of garbage bags—layers of badly stained and almost-purposefully ripped pieces—and once-white rags. His face was covered in hundreds of tiny pink cuts and white stubble, and multiple stitched-up gashes on his scalp overshadowed what was left of his alabaster hair. He let out a primitive groan and feebly stuck his right hand out toward me, his index finger slightly raised. Instinctively, I tried to grab the finger, only to have my mother forcefully yank my other arm and whisk me into the stationery store as if into safety.

My mother explained that this poor man didn't have a home and might have diseases or mental illnesses, and as such, it wasn't safe for us to be close to him. I asked if we couldn't help him get better.

"That isn't a good idea," she said, "for either him or us."

It seemed so unfair that I began to cry. If he got better, I argued, "he could be friends with Grandpa." My mother tried to comfort me, and in time, her love and the Matchbox cars stopped my tears. But more than thirty years later, I can still smell and taste that man's putrid reek and feel his agony; it's as if he is still staring at me. He was the first time I ever encountered suffering, and the sight of it was a deafening lesson that pain and misery were inevitable. Nothing before that moment had ever had such an impact on me, and it was as if part of his suffering was imprinted on me, transferred inside me. It changed the trajectory of my soft, underdeveloped world.

At an age when normal kids were learning to adjust to the harsh realities of losing a great-grandparent or confronting the death of Wiggles, our class guinea pig, I could not. I was too fragile. Such losses crushed me. I became engulfed by them, by the proof of the cruel certainty that everything in this world would die. And so, out of this fear, I began to repeatedly ask everyone around me if they were okay—perplexing to kids, oddly precocious to adults, and concerning to my parents.

They sat me down one day, and my father explained to me the history of mental specialness in our family. "We love you so much, Topher," he began, "and we want you to know that people in our family—like Grandpa Joe and Aunt Hattie—have powers that make them different but extra special. They sometimes skip generations, so you could have those powers too." And so they took me to see a child development specialist.

The office was in the basement of a mildewy prewar apartment that smelled like dank musk mixed with synthetic, flowery perfume, garnished with mothballs. The specialist, a wrinkled woman in her seventies with gray hair tied up in a bun and lipstick on both front teeth, spoke in a slow, genteel American accent. As my eight-year-old self sat on her chaise lounge, I opened up, telling her about my anxiety for others and my worries about the inevitability of death.

"Topher," she replied, "you are an old soul. That you think of such things means you have a unique gift."

She then put me through a series of tests, which indicated an advanced aptitude for reading. If nurtured, she claimed, this aptitude combined with my early emotional intelligence could lead to remarkable things. That day was also the first time I heard the word "Asperger's." From then on, with the encouragement of my parents, I became a reader. Number one on my wish list for that holiday season was the entire bright-red *Encyclopaedia Britannica* set, which I proudly displayed on the Formica bookshelf in my room. At first I feasted mostly on the history of baseball and superheroes, but in time I found my way back into the plight of others, which is how I first discovered the Holocaust and other human atrocities, like Ethiopia's then-current famines. I became obsessed with the idea of suffering children, just like me, not getting the help they desperately needed from the rest of the world. And perplexingly to me, my preoccupation with learning about the macabre—then prose-lytizing about genocide, mass starvation, and other forms of suffering—made it challenging for me to forge friendships with other eight-year-olds.

As elementary school progressed, instinct drove me to be more social, but my continued inability to pick up on age-appropriate small talk and social cues got in the way. And unfortunately, aside from brief moments in the hallways between classes, the only ample opportunity to socialize was in the cafeteria, a wide-open space with extra-long tables under an unevenly painted off-white ceiling and enough reverberating noise to torture the anxious, like me. But what I remember most of the lunchroom was the constant smell of ammonia, generously applied to the linoleum floor by women with hairnets and painted eyebrows.

The whole school ate lunch at the same time, the seating determined by grade, then by class, then by the "cool kids" who ate the institutionally provided lunch versus those—like Song Wong Lee, Ajay, and me—who brought a parent-packed brown bag lunch and were tormented for it. My parents would thoughtfully pack me a no-crust PB&J or a fluffernutter wrapped in foil, along with seasonal fruit and a Capri Sun; Song Won Lee, who wore thick, antifog safety goggles that tied in the back, would eat futomaki sushi and his grandmother's malodorous homemade kimchi; and Ajay, in his Caribbean-accented stutter, always refused to share his curry chicken, which, despite my correction, he insisted on calling chicken curry. Nick, our primary torturer, would announce to the room what we'd been packed for lunch that day, accentuating the first syllable of each word, then swap our desserts with the cafeteria's less desirable ones, only to throw them out in front of us.

Despite the fact that his family hailed from Spain and despite being a few shades paler than me, Nick insisted on calling every Caucasian-looking kid "White Boy," except for me, whom he un-affectionately called "Weird Boy." Despite the ridicule, Song Won Lee and Ajay were happy enough to listen to me scream over the loud, neglected radiator about the plight of children in Bangladesh and the civil war in Somalia, while they conducted speed-spelling contests and debated how to pronounce words like "isthmus" or "colonel" at our Nerd Purgatory table in the farthest reaches of the lunchroom.

Then junior high arrived. The building was only a block away from my elementary school, but it felt like a new solar system to me. It was half a city block, four times the size of my previous school, with kids bused in from many other neighborhoods throughout the city. Despite being easily mistaken for a jail on the outside, it was a place of fond memories on the inside.

On the first day, Dante, a tall, curly-haired, half-Jamaican kid with a starter mustache, who had just moved into my building, fatefully decided to take me into his group of friends, who were as diverse as the Benetton billboards at the time, and with a new ward-robe of exaggeratedly long white T-shirts, baggy jeans, and GAP hoodies, I finally fit in. We took turns spending lunch hours at one another's apartments, and some days we illegally snuck onto roof-tops and mixed wine coolers and malt liquor in paper bags.

Thanks to my newfound confidence and sense of belonging, I even fell in puppy love. Angelina Georgeatis wore her hair pulled back in a tight bun, bright-red lipstick that could be seen for blocks, door-knocker hoop earrings, and rave pants that were wider than anyone else's around. She approached me by saying she had a crush on Marky Mark and I looked a little like him. Our first kiss, initiated by her soon after, was under a basketball net. Petrified with anxiety about performing at this seminal moment, we misaligned our mouths and banged our teeth together, which we blamed on each other to literally save face. For weeks, we spent every second we could grabbing each other's pants as we grinded together on park benches or kissing in freshly painted stairwells or at friends' houses for the short stints anyone's parents were out. The lightning between us was like nothing I had ever imagined. It seemed to obliterate, or at least make up for, every second of discomfort and pain I had ever felt, and it drowned out any bleak or nihilistic feelings I had about the world.

With sectors of my teenage brain lighting up for the first time, a natural, resting smile debuted across my face, and the happiness fed on itself, attracting more friends and girls who thought I looked like a missing member of NSYNC and would follow me home after school or run away giggling when I approached them. My metamorphosis had taken place, but it came with a catch—caught up in this new world, I began cutting class, and my grades plummeted. Once I had failed three classes, Mr. Silverstein, the vice principal, in his low-tier car salesman suit and unironic '80s mustache, brought me into his cramped office and suggested I transfer into a special education program where I would "receive more attention."

While I was shell-shocked and bewildered he thought I should transfer into special ed, dubbed by all as the class for "retards," the ongoing high of my social standing dulled its impact on me. Not so much for my parents, though; having nurtured my early aptitude for reading and my curiosity for history, they flatly refused to accept his "suggestion." In revolt they hired a private educational advo-cate-cum-guidance counselor, who set up an appointment with a learning specialist in Chelsea.

The day of the appointment was dark and drizzly, and my parents met me two blocks away so no one would see us walk up to the green-and-white awning that read "Juvenile Learning Institute." The waiting room was small and sterile, littered with the usual neutral magazines—*Consumer Reports*, *Cosmopolitan*, and *People*—plus a few educationally minded periodicals, which my mother positioned herself next to. I was once again greeted by a woman in her late seventies with a polite face and more wrinkles in the leathery real estate of her neck than I thought possible.

Yellow tungsten lights gave off a constant institutional buzz as the woman administered a series of Rorschach, index card association, and multiple-choice tests. She told me so often that "it's okay if you don't know an answer" that I believed her and was eventually told, "You have ADD and a cognitive processing disorder, which, while we don't know why, is becoming more and more common." Having no reference point for what this meant, I asked if this would affect my life in any important ways. "If you plan to have a career in a field that requires fast cognitive reactions or extensive memorization, it just might." Would my dream of becoming an international civil rights or corporate lawyer who could help those suffering all over the world fit into that category? "Yes," she said, without changing the expression on her face. "I'm sorry, but some people are just not wired for certain things." As those words rolled out of her mouth, the serotonin supply in my brain seemed to instantaneously deplete. I felt nauseous. Sweat materialized on the bottom of my feet and on my palms, and my heartbeat soared, akin to the grisly, panicky feeling of being seasick or smoking way too many bidi cigarettes.

I told her I had no other questions and walked back to the waiting room, where I switched places with my parents. While I was not privy to their conversation, they told me later that night that they were immediately entering me into a private school that would, they assured me, help me focus, nurture my talents, and provide me with the smaller classes, extra tutoring, and special attention I needed and deserved.

Upon hearing this my stomach twanged, followed by a wave of nausea. As dizziness set in, I closed my eyes in an effort to regain balance and felt the bottom drop out of my life. I was in a free fall, and I was certain my new friends, the only group to ever accept me, would soon forget me. Out of sight, out of mind.

While I couldn't identify it at the time, this feeling equal parts hopeless and helpless, was my first anxiety attack.

Chapter 3

A Trillion Little Pieces

ONE OF THE MORE MIND-BENDING ironies of adolescence is how our lack of life experience magnifies the importance of just about everything. A positive experience, like a first kiss, is earth-shattering, but a negative turn, like being pulled away from your friends and first love, is nothing less than the end of the world.

In my case, my world ended with transferring from my diverse downtown public school to a racially, economically, and religiously homogenous, wealthy private school on New York's posh Upper East Side that fast-tracked my teenage brain into a dangerously fragile place.

Compared to my junior high's penitentiary-like facade, the four connected brown- and red-brick luxury townhouses that constituted my new high school were dramatically upscale and almost frighteningly foreign. Inside, the furniture and decor looked lifted from the set of a movie about a plush boarding school, and the younger students (the school spanned kindergarten through high school) wore matching blue-and-white uniforms, while we high school kids could wear whatever we wanted—if we paid a five-dollar fee at the door. Although I was on heavy financial aid, I still paid up, every Monday through Friday.

Up until this time, I had never been exposed to such wealth. My friends and the kids I knew wore baggy clothes and thought of shopping at Eddie Bauer as a splurge. Here, the kids were decked out in DKNY and Armani casual and even formal wear with multithousand-dollar purses on their arms. They all had the same ski-sloped noses and neon sports cars and even smelled different. There wasn't a whiff of ammonia in the air; these hallways and classrooms carried the expensive aroma of lemon and lavender combined with sweet perfume, musky cologne, and salon-worthy gels—all gratuitously applied.

I was intimidated, and right on day one, my heart palpitations kicked in as I assured myself that, as a downtown kid, I would never belong here, rejecting my new environment before it could reject me. But despite my dismissive body language, my soft, stuttering voice broadcasted the truth: surrounded by overdressed, gorgeous, pixie-faced girls and boys with even more extravagant outfits and even prettier hair—all of whom ignored my existence—I was as envious as anyone could ever be.

I was seeing Angelina and my public school friends less and less, and because they were always together, my weekends-only appearances began to reek of desperation. As both my anxiety and teenage hormones increased, my normal adolescent pimple problem transformed into severe acne. I would awake, check the mirror, and stare in disbelief at the horror of puss-filled whiteheads organizing on my face. Gone was the "glowing" skin everyone had once envied. I was now a certified member of the disfigured/pockmarked club, and I didn't stand a chance on the Upper East Side.

Across the street from school was a café called Twilight that catered to the most privileged kids. It was a jaunty place: shabby-chic-meets-tropical-meets-baroque, with dark red tablecloths that hung down to the floor and large, leafy plants everywhere. The owner, Matthew, an effeminate fortysomething with round tortoiseshell glasses that he often color coordinated with his cravat, was smitten with the popular kids, naming appetizer specials after them and involving himself in their social dynamics to a suspicious extent.

One Friday, despite my deep social anxiety and with a bout of brash confidence, I convinced myself to eat lunch at Twilight to prove I wasn't intimidated. I got there early, before anyone else, and snagged a table toward the back, far from the "cool kid" sectional adjacent to Marc's maître d' stand. I ordered the tuna tartare salad special and an iced tea, then buried my head in *The Catcher in the Rye*, which I carried around to serve as a talking point to appear interesting, if anyone ever approached me.

Soon enough the two most popular boys at the school, Danny Bronfman and Robbie Larosh, began holding court on the couch. With the same straight haircut, thin lips, angular noses, and defined chins, they could have been related. They were prettier and certainly fancier than any girls I had ever seen.

Between seemingly carefree but perfectly choreographed bites of *steak frites*, Danny continually flipped picture-perfect sandy blond hair out of his eyes and bragged about his father's renowned plastic surgery practice, which, already famous for its nose jobs, was now branching into acne treatments the good doctor had invented. Sinking his teeth into a panini, Robbie, dressed in a fitted camel-colored leather jacket, pressed black slacks, and matching equestrian-inspired dress boots, proposed offering up classmates as guinea pigs, as long as he got a cut of the action. Danny liked the idea, and together they started making a "pizza face list." Without hesitation, Danny suggested "that kid who tries to look ghetto with the baggy jeans and white T-shirts" as—without contest—first on the list.

Did they know I was there and this was an act of cruelty? Or was my presence a mere coincidence? Regardless, every blood cell rushed to my head, causing a headache so pulsating I could temporarily hear my own heartbeat. I was paralyzed and felt my hands go clammy. I closed my eyes and saw colors in what I imagined a bad trip must be like. I pulled out of my bag my portable CD player and the five-dollar sunglasses I had purchased on the street, put them on, and pretended to read *The Catcher in the Rye* as I fought back tears with every iota of self-respect I possessed. I didn't make a sound, but all my efforts could not stop the tears that streamed down the mountain range of swollen sores cluttering my face and soaked what was indeed my white T-shirt.

From this moment on, barely a second went by that I didn't think about my—and everyone else's—complexion, assessing the size and shape of pores and counting imperfections, even using a mathematical formula to compare others' to mine. It was a debilitating obsession. I spent countless hours in front of any mirror I could find, analyzing how different types of light or angles might lessen the severity of my acne, but it was all futile. No matter what I did, my skin defined me. Each new or particularly bad breakout, which, from start to finish, tended to last about a week, was hauntingly followed by another eruption—so the clear-up I so desperately wished for never arrived.

I hadn't seen Angelina in months, and I wanted to keep it that way. I was embarrassed of my acne to the point that I was relieved when she repeatedly brushed me off. Then, suddenly, she became obsessed with meeting Emmett, our family's newly adopted golden Persian cat. So on a Saturday afternoon, when my parents were at their almost-weekly off-off-Broadway matinee, Angelina hit the buzzer downstairs, and nausea butterflies assaulted my stomach, forcing me to repeatedly swallow my spit so I could regain composure. I opened the door, and as she walked in, I saw her eyes dart instantly to the crowd of red mounds near my chin, which I heard someone in my neighborhood describe as "an acne goatee." Once her brain had registered this new information, she made direct eye contact and kissed me. An uncomfortably pregnant pause followed the kiss—a pause unacknowledged but mutually understood.

We sat together on the couch, while Angelina petted Emmett, who rolled onto his back, demanding and duly receiving our undivided attention. Only after he was satisfied with having his belly and face rubbed profusely did he hop away, leaving us sitting side by side. I put on *Big Fish*, which I knew Angelina wanted to see, and we were soon hugging, spooning, then briefly kissing before she pulled her face away abruptly and planted her mouth between my neck and shoulder. I felt her eyelashes tickle my neck, then a tear roll down my skin. In a cracking voice, I asked, "Why are you crying?"

"Because I love you so much," she said.

"Isn't that a good thing?"

"Topher, I love you, but I'm not in love with you anymore."

My heart sank. "I don't understand," I said, gasping between words. "I'm confused."

After a long pause, she said, "I will always love and care about you, but as a friend from now on."

"Then why were you just kissing me?"

"Because I love you and will miss the shit out of you." Her tears now flowed steadily, soaking the collar of her red-and-white long-sleeved Tommy Hilfiger polo.

"You said I was your star—that your world would revolve around me. Why did you say that if you didn't mean it?" I was crying, but I was angry.

"Don't make this any harder for me." Angelina hugged me then. "If you love me, you'll support me and my decision."

"But why did you lie to me?"

"Stop being so mean!" Her voice rose. "Can't you see I'm suffering too? That I'll always love you, even when we're broken up?"

We stopped speaking but stayed locked in a hug, holding each other tight and sobbing, creating an almost-amusing echo. I kept trying to look into her eyes, and she kept turning her head, either to deflect my gaze or to avoid the grotesque condition of my skin. After what felt like hours, Angelina popped up and, without looking directly at me, put on her coat, walked to the door, and stiffly said, "I have to go home and help my sister with her homework."

I guess she forgot it was the weekend.

A few weeks later, on the way home from school, I cut through Stuyvesant Town, the eighty-acre residential complex on Manhattan's east side where my public school friends and I used to hang out. And there they were, sitting on benches near the basketball courts and drinking out of brown paper bags. I smiled, temporarily overcome with nostalgia, until I saw Dante. I noticed he had a much thicker, caterpillar-shaped mustache. I also saw that he was with Angelina. They were sitting sideways on a bench by themselves, looking into each other's eyes, with their legs wrapped around each other's waists.

This betrayal was something I wouldn't fully understand for many years. All I knew at the time was that it ripped open my heart and stamped out whatever adolescent optimism was left. It marked the official end of my innocence, cutting the last string of hope that had been keeping me together. I was ashamed of my appearance, heartbroken at this betrayal, and devastated by the harsh realities of my life. Unable to process the violent feelings of pain, humiliation, disappointment, and disillusionment, I unknowingly ushered myself into a state of numbness.

Much later I would learn how this would impede my capacity to trust others, to see the good in humanity, and to feel good about myself. I would learn the clinical diagnosis for the affliction I suffered as an adolescent was dysthymia, a chronic form of depression that felt like I was in purgatory, overcome by an anguish that wouldn't let up, wouldn't go away. Instead of expressing my feelings, I turned the pain inward. I shut down my emotions and existed on autopilot. I simply did not want to be around others, so I spent all the time I could alone at home, out of sheer self-preservation, holding onto the last bits of functionality I could still muster.

Days dragged into each other in a monotonous haze. I would go to and from school on the bus armed against the world with my headphones. I would attend every class, avoiding my peers as much as humanly possible, and would watch movies, play video games, and sleep the weekends away. Occasionally, I would eat meals with my parents, who went to great lengths to try to connect with me and figure out what I was going through, but I wouldn't budge. I suppose they assumed that whatever was going on was normal— just your average teenage angst—because eventually they let me be.

And since home was the only place I could avoid the pain of social interactions, I bonded with the one entity who was always there, always friendly, and always available—Emmett, our outlandishly fluffy, flat-faced, anime-eyed, golden Persian cat.

Chapter 4

Emmett

BEFORE EMMETT ENTERED MY LIFE, the only exposure I had to animals was petting a pup or chasing a cat at a friend's house or gazing at them through barriers at the Bronx Zoo. As a young kid going through a stage of voracious reading, I found myself studying animals incessantly until I became utterly obsessed with them. I campaigned relentlessly for a furry friend, but my parents repeatedly shot down the idea because our landlord did not allow pets—that is, until the unintended, ruinous effects of taking me out of public school emboldened my parents to rebel against this rule and one day bring home Emmett, a pedigreed golden Persian kitten.

I remember the exact position I was sitting in on the couch when they walked in, jolted me out of my listlessness by announcing they had bought me a cat, and opened the carrier to let him out. Emmett crept forward slowly, twitched his long white whiskers, and scrunched up his perfectly symmetrical face framed by a mane that sprung out in every direction so that he resembled a miniature but lifelike lion cub crossed with a bonsai-sized weeping willow.

Emmett surveyed his surroundings, then approached me fearlessly, leading with his nose. It wiggled, suggesting he was analyzing me, so instinctively, I did the same thing back to him. We locked gazes, mutually analyzing and nose-wiggling, until I moved my nose to the fluff on top of his head and picked him up. Emmett, instead of scurrying away, comfortably maneuvered onto his back like a baby, tilting his head upward and staring at me innocently with oversize, piercing jade eyes.

Our bond was forged. In the midst of my harrowing state of juvenile misery, I was hypnotized by the purity and magnificence of this angelic creature, who, for the first time since I met Angelina, transported me to a blissful place where I simply forgot my pain.

From that moment on, Emmett and I claimed each other as codependents in the household. I discovered his preferred meal—Fancy Feast kitten food—and brushed out his long golden hair daily. In return, he trailed me around and slept above my pillow. When I left for school in the morning, he would follow me to the door, and he would be in the same spot when I got home as if he had waited there for me all day. When I opened the door, no matter how full my arms were, he would demand my undivided attention by aggressively meowing and rubbing his little face on my leg. He would keep this up until I dropped everything, scooped him into my arms, and massaged both sides of that cherubic face as he licked my hand with his sandpaper tongue. Once satiated, Emmett would hop to the floor, run past me in both directions, then settle down, either in a sphinx position or on his back with his belly in the air.

Steering clear of all hurt in my life and staying home with Emmett's cathartic, unconditional affection for and dependence on me was the only light during a time when my entire relationship with the outside world was defined by pain. When I looked into the mirror to brush my teeth, I had to reaccept that this aching, puss-filled war zone was my face, not another nightmare. Every new eruption was physically torturous, but enormously more emotionally punishing—I was certain Angelina left me because she couldn't stand the horror of seeing these grotesque deformities. These wounds festered in my subconscious as proof of humanity's inherent superficiality and lack of integrity. This was a darkness that reverberated through me, a lens through which I colored everything, convinced that everyone from the bus drivers to the overprivileged kids in school were all judging me for my deformity. In reality, they were just going about their days. But in my tunnel of hopelessness, I was sure every person was cruel and disingenuous.

Emmett, though, exemplified the kindness I couldn't find or depend on from any human. He was nonjudgmental—whether by choice or evolution—utterly disinterested in social hierarchy, and totally lacking any ulterior agenda. He didn't care how my skin looked, whether I lived in a doorman building, what labels were on the clothes I wore, if I took a date to prom, or what my parents did for a living. Unlike everyone else I had ever known, he was never hypocritical, never took advantage of me, never forced me to do anything I didn't want to do. I know you're thinking this is because he's an animal, but he just had a way about him. My mother, too, always used to say of Emmett, "I can be having the worst day in the world, but seeing his sweet, fluffy, scrunched-up face always makes me happy."

I see now I was either too emotionally unintelligent or too shell-shocked to properly comprehend that during that excruciating time in my life, this twelve-pound feline was my lifeline. Thinking about him now sends a rush of nostalgia coursing through the synapses of my brain, and heavy, happy tears well behind my eyes.

Emmett lived a very long life—twenty-four human years—and no matter how much time passes, the impact he had on me never fades. Because we didn't speak with words, it's fitting that the immeasurably intimate understanding we shared can't be accurately described through them. But the memories of our sacred bond, his blissful innocence, and his cathartic companionship will always be a part of me, a guardian angel, watching over me now as he did in the torturous growing pains that defined my darkest early days. The thought of him now conjures up the image of his cherubic, weeping-willow, scrunched-up face, and brings a tear to my eyes as I write, but is dwarfed by the nostalgic smile across my face.

Chapter 5

Apocalyptic Adolescent Catastrophes

UNLIKE ALL OTHER LIVING CREATURES, we humans are cursed with huge brains that allow us to comprehend our mortality. We are locked in a battle with time, the most elusive thing about being alive. We can't control time, but our emotional states can change how it's perceived. When we're content or in a flow state or with the right people, time flies, but when we are uneasy, sad, disconnected, withdrawn, the seconds pass like minutes, the minutes like hours, the hours like days that never end.

During my college years, despite the privilege of an out-of-state university experience, time dragged for me. I should have been jumping at the opportunities before me. Instead, I was plagued by unresolved feelings of rejection and resentment, followed by a dark, crippling cloud of social anxiety. Although my skin miraculously cleared and I was physically grown, deep, emotionally suffocating wounds festered inside me, impeding any ability to trust others, understand myself, or have healthy, communicative relationships.

Unresolved emotions are a uniquely human occurrence. Animals, I later learned, don't share our ability to self-reflect, nor are they aware of their mortality, so they act principally on instinct. As a result they can't carry emotional or mental baggage in the way we do. This, according to Robert Sapolsky's ingenious book *Why Zebras Don't Get Ulcers,* makes animals much less susceptible to chronic, stress-related illnesses. If humans could only let go of the baggage we carry and come to terms with our feelings as they happen, or even a little later, instead of ignoring them or sweeping them under the rug, we wouldn't get ulcers either. But we do. We're humans. We don't come to terms with emotions. We ignore and we sweep under the rug, where once-small issues spread like terminal cancer.

The consequences can be devastating, as they were to me. I behaved in ways that betrayed my values and my very sense of self. I felt woefully ashamed of myself, adding more layers onto the armor I wore to cover up just how lost I felt.

Not a great way to start your college experience.

The new-student orientation took place in an Olympic-sized gymnasium, the largest and best outfitted I'd ever seen. Moments after I walked in, however, the cacophony of so many people talking at once triggered an immediate sensory overload, which in turn made my stomach twitch and sent blood rushing into my frontal lobes. As I took deep, measured breaths to regain composure, I observed hundreds of people, all of whom, unlike me, seemed to know one another or, at the very least, seemed to know where to go, what to say, and what to do.

Fear rippled through me, so to temper it, I perverted it into anger, creating an identity—which, looking back, I now see as a debilitating crutch—that I could manage. It was fairly easy: I became an elitist New Yorker and began to size up everybody around me from that superior vantage point. I took in their overly happy faces, brightly colored clothing, and submissive body language and concluded they were either from the suburbs or cities much smaller than my own and were, compared to me, unsophisticated and therefore unworthy. I took comfort from my own dark clothes and persistent scowl, basking in my paper-thin veneer of pseudosuperiority.

It's not lost on me that in high school I had sought solace in rejecting the superficiality and snobbery of those around me, and now, through some power of osmosis, the superficiality and snobbery had become, in a bastardized way, a part of me. Overwhelmed, frightened, and reeling from countless layers of repressed pain, I leaned into my new identity, hiding behind myself.

The intense feelings that ran through me the first night in my dorm room are sensations my body will always vividly remember. After a never-ending first day, riddled with discomfort, I was achingly exhausted. I climbed into the single bed, pulled my red-and-white tablecloth-patterned Kmart comforter over me, and suddenly every inch of my skin felt an intensely icy-hot sensation of pleasure and pain. I curled my limbs into a cocoon, scrunched my eyes closed, and watched as dark shapes materialized and bright colors flickered up from the floor. Drifting off, I felt a fleeting moment of peace, which temporarily took me back to my bed at home, in my parents' apartment, with Emmett by my side—a place where I didn't have to interact with anyone. But as I descended into sleep, I could not stop thinking about the inferno of new monsters I would be forced to interact with the next day.

My first and closest college friendships were formed through sheer proximity; Adam, Patrick, and I, by chance, lived on the same floor of our freshman dorm. After surveying the others nearby—a Japanese student who barely spoke English, an activist who plastered "Go Vegan" stickers on his door, a spiked-collar enthusiast who worshipped Marilyn Manson, and a good ol' boy who hung the Confederate flag out his window—our triumvirate was formed.

Adam, a soft-spoken kid from the DC suburbs, was the polar opposite of me. He was tall and boyishly handsome with short, gelled-back curly black hair. He wore striped kindergarten-esque crewnecks, bleached dad jeans, and oversize New Balance sneakers. In contrast to my perma-scowl, Adam's exuberant, welcoming smile offered wholesomeness, which, combined with his charisma and ability to read social cues, made him captivating in a wholly unique way.

Patrick, with ruddy hair and a matching complexion, was also perpetually happy. He was from Sedona, Arizona, stood a head and a half shorter than Adam, and had an unlimited reserve of energy. He thrived on attention, often playing harmless but elaborate jokes on complete strangers. He incessantly quoted *Lethal Weapon* and other late-'80s action movies, loved top-forty music, and viewed the world like an innocent.

They were sheltered, suburban mama's boys, so my darkness, cynicism, and New York attitude gave them an edge they lacked, and while I would perpetually mock them for it, their cheery dispositions, smiling faces, brightly colored clothing, and positive outlook on life reminded me of who I once was—and so desperately still wanted to be. (I would later come to realize animals can do the same thing for us that these friends did for me—help us rediscover our innocence.) We brought one another closer to who we thought we needed to be. Formed under pressure, our union made us instant family—Adam the innocent, Patrick the energetic, and Topher the anxiously angry—and provided the safety blankets required to face this expansive and intimidating new world.

As time passed and the initial shock of our new environment wore off, we learned campus social life was dominated by Greek life, and the houses were defined by reputation: the Good Ol' Boys, the Slackers, the African Americans, and the Fratty Frat Boys, the wildest and cockiest of the bunch, who threw the best parties and got the most girls. This fraternity was full of kids from the Northeast, mainly from the Five Towns of Long Island and wealthy New Jersey suburbs—guys known for being especially loud, arrogant, and affluent. When the recruiting season began, word got around about the freshman with a big New York City attitude, and as befitted their reputation, the Fratty Frat Boys set their sights on me.

Feeling as rudderless as ever, with a deep-seated yearning to belong, I jumped at the opportunity, as long as they took my two smiling suburban friends as well.

Without hesitating, we became pledges of the fraternity, undergoing myriad bouts of ritualized hazing to become "brothers." The older members, who had once been subjected to the very same treatment, organized everything from drinking competitions to emotional degradation, sleep deprivation, and occasionally vile acts that people like me will always be too humiliated to share and, no matter how hard we try, can never forget. It was a juvenile, testosterone-filled twenty-first-century tribal initiation for the overprivileged.

At the time, experiencing crippling social anxiety and feeling hopelessly numb, I didn't have the emotional intelligence to admit this. To distract myself, and to feel *something*, I embraced the emotional and physical pain; this not only helped me foster an identity but also provided proof that I was alive. While the emotionally healthy, like Adam and Patrick, struggled, I leaned in, the model pledge, outdoing everyone, and thus demonstrating my mastery of masculine one-upmanship. What were crowning achievements then, but humiliating memories now, resulted in thrusting myself into verbal and physical conflicts with older members of a rival fraternity and walking away with an unquestioned victory in a put-a-lit-cigarette-between-your-arms-to-see-who-flinches-first race.

These behaviors, however haunting now, solidified my reputation as someone not to be messed with, both inside and outside of the frat. As with most angry, emotionally damaged, suffering individuals, this shell, the armor with which I faced others, was a self-defense mechanism aimed at deflecting and, above all, denying the intense pain I was feeling inside.

At the start of sophomore year, Adam, Patrick, and I—now full-fledged fraternity brothers—moved into the frat house. Although social anxiety still tormented me, I found myself distracted from its discomfort with the enthusiasm of belonging, for the first time since my public high school, to a group. It made everything else feel manageable.

After a while, however, I soon realized Adam, Patrick, and the other fraternity brothers who had become friends had found girlfriends and made other social connections. Instead of being happy for them, I saw this as a betrayal, as if they had deserted me. Once again I found myself becoming increasingly desperate and began to analyze everything about myself and everyone around me.

As a distraction I threw myself into the fraternity's group activities, namely the hazing of new members. Being on the other side, however, I was struck with disgust and could not escape the realization that I had been and still was a part of this.

Something snapped. I felt like I was waking up, not just to the toxic masculinity but to the similarity it all bore to the superficial, hypocritical, and materialistic behavior that had plagued me in high school.

With Adam and Patrick now having the time of their lives, I knew I couldn't express my revulsion to them, so I kept everything inside. I filled the void—the "loss" of my friends—with work, diving into my new job tending bar at Bertucci's Brick Oven Pizza on Thursday, Friday, and Saturday nights as well as my philosophy and sociology classes.

Armed with Nietzsche's *Thus Spoke Zarathustra*, I declared everyone in Greek life "conformist hypocrites" who, as I had once been, were asleep and needed to be awakened. I began to write my own poetry and to construct my own manifesto—both assignments for my creative writing class—to satirize the behavior of these pathetically inferior beings. I identified patterns of groupthink in which fraternity and sorority members drank to escape reality; took advantage of their rich parents who paid for their college education, fancy dinners, and BMWs; were unfaithful to their boyfriends and girlfriends; and continually denounced homophobia. In my mind, these revelations also explained why I wasn't happy in this environment, wasn't embraced by the girls on campus, wasn't popular.

I took on the role of a modern, collegiate Martin Luther and preached to inebriated college students over the pounding bass lines, condemning the duplicity and immortality of their behavior and their refusal to question the meaning of life. At first they thought I was joking, based on my previous frat-boy behavior. Then they began calling me insane. Like wildfire, a rumor spread across the entire campus that I had had a mental breakdown. While Adam, who was my roommate at the time, and Patrick, still a true friend, remained loyal, almost everyone else backed away. They told me how Brian Biederman, a senior who had hazed me the hardest, was so angry I had attacked him for being homophobic that, in retaliation, he started a rumor that my breakdown was a result of me coming out as gay.

Knowing that the biggest taboo in this ultramasculine environment was being gay, I decided to use Biederman's move as an opportunity to declare war on the entire system. I lay low until rush, when we put on a huge show to recruit new members. Then, right as the event was in full swing, I emerged from my room and took center stage in full drag—bright-red lipstick and a skintight white dress. After flouncing around and nonchalantly interacting with freshmen who, like I was just the year before, were desperate to find a brotherhood, I climbed on top of a chair in the middle of the main room and delivered an impassioned speech.

"Future friends, it's so serendipitous to have you with us. This day marks our esteemed organization's evolutional revolution, from a fraternity of toxic misogynists to philanthropic, Good Samaritan humanitarians who will raise money for charities; embrace people of all races, cultures, sexual orientations, and creeds; and do everything in our power to help the human race. God bless Pi Kappa Alpha, and God bless you!" Then I gave the crowd an exaggerated air kiss, smacking "smooch" sound and all.

As expected, my fraternity brothers did not take kindly to my performance. In fact, every movement in the room stopped, and the most senior members hustled me away into my room.

Not long after, they held a chapter meeting about the incident and accused me of deliberately sabotaging the sanctity of their letters. While they had no authority to enact a formal punishment, since I still lived in the house, I was fully ostracized. Apart from Adam, Patrick, and a few others who felt sorry for me yet kept their distance, I was now completely surrounded by beer-chugging, weightlifting, trigger-happy enemies.

Living silently in a hostile environment where I was continually taunted became impossible. Having no one to empathize with—no one who held my same steadfast beliefs—began to take a heavy toll on my psyche. As I grew increasingly desperate, I began to feel trapped, enraged. I was losing control. I put these feelings into my writing and excelled in my classes, despite the incessant pounding music and partying that made writing and studying nearly impossible. And any time I requested someone turn down the volume at night, it was instantly turned up instead.

One night a few older members, sensing my frustration, and led, not surprisingly, by Biederman, decided to rig a speaker directly outside my window. With the party at its peak and the speaker blasting full-bore into my window, I flew into a primal rage, jumping onto the deck and ripping out the entire sound system, stunning the party into silence and stopping all the movement on the patio, which was packed wall to wall. As the booing and name-calling ensued, the biggest of my fraternity brothers surrounded me, picked me up, and carried me into the attic, which was used as the chapter room. There, ten brothers took to berating and humiliating me until Michael, drunker than I had ever seen him, stumbled into me, his face a few inches from mine.

"What happened?" he screamed. "You used to be a tough guy!"

"Get the fuck out of my face, you vapid, tacky, nouveau riche Long Island douche canoe," I spat. "All you do is spend your parents' money and brag."

"Not my fault you have to bartend at Bertucci's and drive a Buick," he responded.

"At least I have original thoughts, unlike your conformist, ass-kissing, human cattle meat brain. If you didn't have a BMW and your parents' credit cards, no one in this room would want anything to do with you."

"And do you think anyone here likes you? You belong in a mental institution. Everyone is worried you'll have a breakdown. They're all scared of you, except for me," he replied, then challenged me to a fight.

The crowd parted, giving us space, and in a blurred frenzy, I used my fists to pummel Michael's face again and again and again until we were pried apart.

My hands were bright red, and my clothes were ripped. Michael was cowering on the floor, his face badly bloodied. I didn't really know, nor could I comprehend, what had just happened or how badly he was hurt, but I soon realized I was both crying and hyperventilating while Adam was rubbing my back and trying to talk me down.

Then I heard the sirens—whether it was the campus police or local cops I didn't know.

Chapter 6

Quarter-Life Clichés

IT'S A PECULIAR THING THAT our instincts are perpetually in conflict with the rationality of our oversize brains. The moment we become aware of our existence, this struggle, the very core of what makes us human, takes effect; it serves as the impetus for both the miracles we achieve and the catastrophes we cause. And contrary to what we'd like to think—because it reminds us we are part of nature, not above it—our instincts always win. These gigantic, cosmic magnets, at the last second, scoop up the rational arguments in our brains so we yield over and over again. Proof of this is the universality of our life stages: birth, infancy, toddlerhood, childhood, then the quarter-life crisis that defines the transition between childhood and adulthood. We, unfortunately, cannot reach maturity without going through this clichéd time of unique and complete existential angst.

Which brings us to the next part of my story.

As is common for twenty-one-year-olds, I thought no one could ever understand my intense desire to find myself, that this yearning, like the appreciation of Nietzsche and Pink Floyd, was, clearly, wholly unique to me.

I felt destined to explore the same strange lands as my literary heroes—George Orwell, Joseph Campbell, Hunter S. Thompson, and William S. Burroughs—whose work opened up a pathway to an outside world and a hope of who I could become. Through their adventures, which introduced a plethora of different types of people, places, cultures, and subcultures, I found optimism that a universe beyond claustrophobic campus life existed, which increased the chances somehow, somewhere, I could find a place to fit in, or even thrive.

As silly as it sounds, following their adventure trajectories, through visceral engagement in worldly experiences, my hope was to find the country, culture, ethos where I belonged, magically metamorphosing me from an unemployed, debt-ridden college grad into the next great American author. Regardless of the outcome, at the risk of seeming over overprivileged, graduating and leaving a campus full of people who despised me felt like the best thing to ever happen to me.

To the chagrin of my parents, who wanted me to work and pay off my huge loans, and to the bewilderment of Adam and Patrick, who charitably invited me to join their summer backpacking trip through Europe, I was determined to travel alone. With money saved from bartending, I purchased a one-way ticket from JFK to

Tangier, Morocco, where Burroughs had lived and where both Jack Kerouac and Mark Twain had famously visited, and was off to follow in the footsteps of great writers and to, hopefully, join in their greatness.

After an overnight, double-layover flight, I arrived—hungry, anxious, and bleary-eyed—into the sunshine to find a taxi. Instantly, I was descended upon by seven middle-aged, mustachioed men wearing nightgown-style dresses and yelling at me in Arabic. With auditory overload combined with panic-stricken fear, hunger, and lack of sleep, I hastily sought refuge with the tallest man, who also happened to be screaming a few words in English. With a scowl of contempt, he led me to his taxi while yelling angrily at the other men who had approached me. I opened my *Lonely Planet* guidebook and pointed to the address of the hotel I had chosen, in the oldest part of the city. Stone-faced, my driver nodded, and we began the bumpy half-hour ride.

But instead of a hotel, we ended up in a musty, low-ceilinged rug shop. Feeling awkward and more than a little scared, but seeing no other choice, I followed the proprietor, a portly, bald man with blackened front teeth, through a tunnel to a cavernous room with rugs covering every inch of the walls and ancient antiques cluttering every surface, making me feel uncomfortably claustrophobic.

I was encouraged to sit down on a makeshift wooden seat and given a glass of exorbitantly sweetened mint tea. At this point the proprietor began his show. Despite his age and body shape, he exhibited an acrobatic skill that might have won him a spot in Cirque du Soleil as he lifted and unrolled enormous rug after enormous rug, pausing only briefly to look at me and, on occasion, to pridefully stroke his mustache. Only when the entire wood-and-dirt floor was completely covered with rugs did my disgruntled driver reappear, shouting, "Yela! Buy! Yela! Yela!"

At that moment, sleep-deprived, sweating profusely, and now frightened beyond belief, I realized this trip was one huge mistake. Rather sheepishly, I fumbled for my passport fanny pack, which I kept around my neck, and handed the shopkeeper forty American dollars. Still scowling and now grunting, my driver walked out, my new purchase over his shoulder. I scrambled to my feet and scurried after him. He didn't say another word, just drove to what I hoped would be my hotel in the old city and not another excruciating extortion.

Drenched in sweat, I grabbed the hand crank to roll down the window, and it broke off, right into my hand. With deliberate casualness, I held it in place until we arrived—with a rug and without a handle—at my hotel. I checked in, was led to a musty room that faced a medieval-looking courtyard, climbed into the rigid bed, and fell asleep.

When I awoke hours later, confused in the darkness, I felt my way to the sink next to the bed and pulled a string to the old-fashioned light over the mirror. At once I saw dark, twitching shapes scattering across the mirror—cockroaches, so many that I couldn't even see my reflection. Panicked, I grabbed a Birkenstock sandal and slapped at the mirror, only to see yellowish-white eggs scatter everywhere, some falling into the sink.

On the verge of vomiting, I called for the manager, who combated the roaches with noxious fumes and showed me to a new room. Heart still pounding, I stared up at the new ceiling fan, analyzing the different shapes the mold around it might symbolize, and asked myself why I had taken this torturous trip.

Eager to escape the palace of pestilence, I decided to take a walk the next day and wandered around aimlessly yet cautiously, feeling as if I had discovered a time warp. Every building had been carved from stone, and the entire city was surrounded by a medieval castle wall. Men were holding hands and wearing dresses, while most of the women covered their faces. A harsh light cast elongated shadows and gave everything and everyone an eerie sense of timeless romance. The smells of mint tea, cumin, saffron, and paprika seemed to emanate around every corner, bombarding my senses. The call to prayer, which blared on rickety loudspeakers five times a day, reminding Muslims to pray, though jarring, made me feel enjoyably insignificant in this strange new world I had awakened to.

But what thrilled me most was the sheer abundance of cats. They were everywhere: lounging in the hotel, crossing the town square, wandering in the markets, sleeping on rooftops or pillars, blocking doorways as if they owned the place. And they all looked healthy, feasting on bowls of food and water lining the streets. I was hit with a deep and desperate yearning for Emmett and took solace in bonding with these hundreds of angelic animals. I fed them, earned their trust, became their friend. I learned that Muslim culture, and Morocco in particular, held cats to be sacred, and I knew that being here was, after all, the right decision. Cat people understood the intangible basics of being alive that only these sacred animals could teach us. Emmett would approve, so these had to be my people.

With no itinerary and no obligation to consider anyone else's needs or desires, I zigzagged across the country, stopping in small towns highlighted in the guidebook, exploiting the freedom to do whatever I wanted. Traveling mostly by economy-class train, I encountered modest yet curious people who, despite their circumstances, gave off an aura of contentment I longed to achieve.

They were a benevolent people too. During one of the longest and most crowded train rides I had taken, I had run out of food. I began to feel lightheaded and rather sick. A five-year-old girl who was smushed into the small seat next to me must have noticed because she pulled from her sack a hardboiled egg and, without speaking but with a smile, opened her tiny fingers and handed it to me. I accepted it as graciously as I knew how, then wolfed it down. The little girl's father explained to me that caring for visitors—giving them food or even the shirt off your back—is an essential tenet of Islam, the observance of which can offer an eternal reward. This small gesture so many years ago, made by a such a young person with no ulterior motive, is one I look back on often. It renewed my faith in humanity, affirmed meaning in my life, and filled me with pride to be living in this complicated world.

My heart was soaring and my smile was wide as I arrived in Marrakech. I wandered around Medina, the old town's center, famed for its snake charmers, storytellers, and vendors selling sheep brains, and stopped at a restaurant for the local delicacy, tagine and mint tea. A young man at the next table introduced himself as Abdullah and struck up a conversation, explaining that he wanted to practice his English. He told me about his customs and gave me his opinion on Islam (he wasn't a believer) and on the king of Morocco (he was ambivalent). Then he asked me countless questions about America. Ecstatic I had made a genuine connection with a man my age, I enthusiastically accepted his invitation to join him on a hike in the Berber mountains the following morning.

We set off up a beautiful mountain path where we soon spotted monkeys; Abdullah grabbed hold of my hand, which took me aback, but since I had seen how commonplace it was in this culture, I accepted it. We climbed higher until we arrived at a magnificent waterfall, and Abdullah promptly stripped and jumped into the swimming hole without missing a beat. We spent the rest of the morning comparing our cultures, while inwardly I relished in the purity of connecting with someone from a vastly different background and finding so many commonalities between us. Joseph Campbell, I felt sure, would have approved.

But right when my elation had reached its height, Abdullah pivoted abruptly and asked me to pay him for his time. I was both taken aback and offended. I thought we were friends, and friends did not pay each other for company. Abdullah responded with specific rates of a tour guide, arguing he had educated me about the surroundings and his culture and proclaiming friends wouldn't take advantage of each other either.

When I told Abdullah I had almost run out of money, he nodded in acknowledgment, then asked if I had anything else to offer—perhaps my knee-length Billabong board shorts.

I was saddened by his quick reversal but even more offended and countered bitterly that money was the root of all evil and brought out the worst in people.

"You Americans think you're so great, that you piss out Coca-Cola." Then he spit in my direction, intentionally missing me.

Abdullah and I went our separate ways without saying another word, and when I finally arrived at my hotel after hours of retracing my steps alone, my feet were a misery of puss-filled blisters.

It was true, the money was running out, and with no way to work in a country whose language I did not speak, I used my remaining cash to get to London, banking on my experience as a bartender at Bertucci's Brick Oven Pizza to earn my rent.

Twenty-eight pubs later, I was hired.

But one evening was all it took to derail everything. I was cleaning ashtrays when two drunk Middle Eastern men wearing chest-hair-baring silk shirts yelled for my attention. When I failed to promptly respond, one began dropping his smoked cigarettes on the floor and, in broken English, demanded I clean it up.

Instantly, this flipped a switch in me, and without pause, I dumped the entire tray of ashes I had been collecting onto the two men. Dumbfounded at first, they recovered quickly and came at me. I held my ground until I was escorted out by my short, stocky boss who had often bragged about serving time and who, after yelling at me at the top of his lungs, spit flying, fired me on the spot.

Serendipitously, the week before I had developed a deep bond with two construction workers I had served, and they had offered me work if I ever needed it. So I called them, and the next day I was on their crew, painting, laying floors, and even pouring concrete, all of which I had no idea how to do.

Aware I was saving for my next trip—to India, in honor of Joseph Campbell—they always treated me to pints after work. I was once again struck by the kindness of strangers in a foreign land. They gave work to a kid with no construction experience and whom they barely knew. They taught me that the true test of character is how one acts toward someone who can't benefit them in any way. And they gave me time to squirrel away a few thousand pounds to book my one-way trip to Mumbai on Bangladesh Airlines.

Minutes after disembarking from the cramped flight, I was met by men in military uniforms holding rifles that looked so old I thought they were muskets. Then, once again at the mercy of a taxi driver who didn't speak English, I spent an hour-long ride praying he would take me to the destination I had pointed to in my guidebook, slack-jawed at the chaos around us: countless near-accidents, nonstop honking, and unfinished construction projects on every block. The streets were strewn with garbage and giant spools of unruly telephone wire, and the smells seemed to change by the second, ranging from sweet flowers and sweeter jasmine to burning plastic and the lingering sulfuric smell of open sewers, which remained in my nose long after we passed.

I was so desperate from hunger and sleep deprivation when we arrived that I didn't even care that the dilapidated building lacked any hint it was actually a hotel. Bent under the weight of my humongous backpack, I followed my driver into the desolate lobby, up stuffy staircase after staircase, and through a door to a decaying, garbage-strewn tar roof.

When the door closed behind us, the gravity of this situation hit me, and panic set in. This was Morocco all over again. I felt my back become drenched in sweat, and my bowels pulsed, as I anticipated his cohorts bursting out from their hideouts, covering my face with chloroform, removing my kidney, then pondering whether to mutilate me or just leave me naked in an alley for sport.

Whether it was his own fight-or-flight reflexes kicking in or my twisted facial expression that caused it, my driver's baby face contorted, and sensing his own danger, he shot his hands up and yelled what seemed to be the only English word he knew: "*Help!*"

My bag dropped as my own hands went up, as each of us, through painfully awkward pantomime communication, aimed to let the other know neither of us was a threat. Minutes later, after shaking hands and cautiously laughing it off, we found someone on the street who showed us the hotel across the way, and I was soon in a tiny room, snuggled up on a paper-thin mattress, sleeping off the jet lag and near-death experience, which was really an innocent miscommunication my ethnocentric instincts misread.

The following day, I set out to explore the oldest neighborhoods of Mumbai. Even though I grew up in New York City, I had never seen so many people—particularly children—begging. I found it heartbreaking beyond words. They were plagued by diseases I had never encountered before. Gigantic growths of elephantiasis obscured their faces, and reptilian-looking scales covered their skin. These suffering souls with their sorrowful eyes resembled animals trapped in cages—reminders of human fragility, of mortality, of the inherent unfairness and cruelty of the world.

Yet juxtaposed with this deep anguish was also a gaiety. I was struck by bright colors everywhere. Women wore vivid traditional clothing, and rich hues managed to peek through every wall's layers of rust and dirt. The streets and sidewalks were packed with rickshaws that nearly ran over a drove of uniformed school children, celebratory processions of entire families throwing ropes of flowers, oxen pulling carts, and people racing to their next destination, dodging others who were asleep, bathing, and transporting wares on their heads.

And then there were the cows—the mothers, the providers of milk—which, gloriously to me, had the right of way over both human and vehicular traffic. Seeing these large, beautiful animals walk wherever they wanted through the most modern human creations thrilled me. Little wonder someone who was saved by, worshipped, and most dearly missed his cat brother had his heart stolen by India.

The city was alive, in constant motion, and perhaps for the first time since I was a child, I felt exhilaratingly alive. Every sense was possessed by what I observed to be the opposite of the societal norms and rules of my own culture, and this stimulation of my sensory faculties made me feel like I had no limits, that anything was possible.

I was happy and welcoming in a way I had never been before, and people often approached me with friendly curiosity. Some just wanted to say hi, while others wanted to touch my hair, take a photo with me, practice their English, or hear what I thought of their country. Surface-level as these interactions may have been, I felt an inexplicable joy from these people. I saw it in the slight twinkle in their eyes, which saw through to the irony of being alive and led me to believe Indians are silent insiders on the big cosmic joke, having accepted there's no meaning of life.

With my spirits running high, I even took my parents up on their suggestion to visit a local holy man recommended to them by a friend they had still kept in touch with from their hippie ashram days in the 1960s. I took the elevator to the top floor of a high-rise office building and walked down a brightly lit, stale hallway, and just as I pressed the buzzer, it swung open. A disheveled Indian man, dressed in a once-white, oversize suit with matted shoulder-length hair, slid past me as I inhaled a putrid smell of onions, sweat, and rotting cheese.

"Come in!" yelled a heavily accented male voice.

I followed his voice down a hallway and into a living room that resembled a staged corporate office. From the wrinkles around his eyes, he looked to be in his eighties. He was bald with loose cheeks, drooping earlobes, and a long gray beard, which flowed elegantly down his loose orange robe—the standard uniform of holy men, or sadhus.

My sadhu was seated on a wide, heavily creased brown leather couch in front of a large open window letting in a breeze that did little to counter the sweltering heat and lack of air-conditioning. After I accepted his invitation to sit, he grabbed my right hand with both of his and stared into my eyes. Without saying a word, he somehow made this feel like a test.

A middle-aged Indian woman then approached, interrupting us to bring the sadhu a cup of water in a metal glass. The sadhu nodded, then handed the cup to me. I was already feeling excruciatingly uncomfortable, so not wanting to be rude, I took a small sip and placed the cup down. After several minutes of silence that felt like hours to me, the sadhu asked if I was American. I nodded, and following another uncomfortably pregnant pause, he told me he could feel the sadness in me.

"Sorrow only exists," he said, "because we affirm it in our minds, so we must learn how to deny it with our minds. Central to this is making others happy because, like hate, which happiness exceeds in strength, it gets doubled or even tripled when it's shared."

I was just about to open my mouth when I heard the buzzer. He held up a hand, apologized for cutting our meeting short, and asked if I could spare a donation for the poor man I saw on the way in. I handed him a handful of rupees, and we walked to the door.

That night I went to bed peacefully, thinking of all I'd already learned in my short time in India. There was no warning of the sharp, pulsating stomach pains or nausea that suddenly woke me up. I stood, doubled over, and half crawled, half stumbled to the waste basket just in time to empty my stomach. I then crawled to the toilet, where liquid spewed in every direction, as my face contorted, one hand grasping my stomach, the other punching the floor in a feeble attempt to distract or more evenly distribute the astonishing pain. Time became obsolete. My wretched, fevered body heaved for an undetermined amount of time. As I drifted in and out of consciousness, I could think of nothing but that the source of this misery could only be the cup of water at the holy man's office.

I worked up the energy to stand and make my way to the door but collapsed once I reached it. I accepted this new position and fell asleep right there until I was assaulted by the putrid smell of ammonia coming from the hallway, which made me violently vomit all over again. Peeking through the gap in the door, I saw a mop swiveling only a few feet from my face. In desperation, I sat up and opened the door, coming face to face with an older man in a cleaning uniform who seemed as horrified by the sight of me as I was of him. I begged him to stop cleaning with words he couldn't understand, shut the door, collapsed, then vomited once more.

When I finally came to, a man I assume was a hotel employee and who spoke good enough English, was asking if I had money for a doctor.

"Yes," I managed, and he ran off, returning shortly with a middle-aged man in a suit. This man reached into a black medical bag and pulled out a pen-sized flashlight. He peeked into my throat, let out a frustrated yell in Hindi, then furiously shook the flashlight, showing me the battery was dead.

For the next two days, I shed alarming amounts of fluids, was unable to keep anything down, and suffered hallucinations that made me feel hopeless. For the first time in my life, I feared I might die. I placed a collect call to my parents, who were able to locate a doctor affiliated with the American Embassy who diagnosed me with amoebic dysentery, gave me an extrastrong antibiotic, and sent me on my way.

But even as I waited for the medication to take hold, the mere sight and smell of Indian food repelled me, and I continued to lose weight. In the greatest irony for someone who had come to India to find an authentic, *un*-American experience, my saving grace became eating at Mumbai's one McDonald's, the only food my body could recognize.

The days turned into weeks, and while my fever dissipated and McDonald's had soothed my stomach, intermittent nausea lingered, and my hotel bill was adding up.

I had wanted to experience other worlds, find myself, reveal life's meaning, and be inspired to write the next great novel. Instead, I was overwhelmed with fear that my sickness would never subside. I had no other choice but to go home to New York City and live with my parents, a total and utter failure.

A transformative hero's journey into adulthood indeed.

Chapter 7

Spiraling Down

IT IS PERHAPS NO SURPRISE that as the only living beings capable of reasoning, complex language, and introspection, we see ourselves as the center of the universe. This selfish mindset enables another uniquely human trait, our egos, which, combined with our ingenuity, allow us to create civilization and all the intricate beauty that makes our lives meaningful and worth living. But along with all the glories come equally excessive pitfalls: harsh letdowns, emotional turbulence, and melancholy. By believing the world revolves around us, we see things as *we* are, instead of how things actually are. So when the world comes crashing down, in our minds, the fault falls squarely on our shoulders, brutally crushing dreams and leaving us disillusioned with the world and in a feedback loop of humiliation and misery. This is exactly where I found myself after my failed voyage of self-discovery, when, instead of writing the "next great novel," I was beset with amoebic dysentery, debt-ridden, and living in my parents' rent-controlled apartment in New York—

back where I had started.

In all my travels, I wasn't able to write. I created nothing apart from a few stream-of-consciousness journal entries. It's not that I didn't try. I did—and I failed. There was no novel, no publishing contract. Only $30,000 of student debt, unemployment, and my childhood bedroom.

There was one saving grace, though—my beautiful, furry savior.

When I arrived home, before I even hugged my parents or took off my overstuffed, tattered backpack, Emmett ran to me, and I embraced his little body, stuck my face in his neck, and took a giant whiff of his freshly licked fur. He rubbed his face into mine as he purred, first a slow murmur, then a full-on motorboat hum. I dropped to the floor as I massaged his little body, which felt more brittle than I remembered, and momentarily forgot the stomach cramps, nausea, and seemingly random jarring pains.

That night, as the spasms became worse, I found myself bent in half, moaning, and clawing at my shoulders in a fruitless attempt to redistribute the pain, when Emmett, who had retaken his position at the top of my bed, hopped closer to me and rubbed his body against my shoulder, using it as a scratching post. Instinctively, I ran my fingers through his long, thick fur as he stared up at me with those wide, empathetic eyes. Once again, only his affection was able to soothe me, and at this realization, I began to weep with guilt for having abandoned him for my catastrophically untransformative voyage. I could only stare back at him as I both apologized and promised to never leave him again.

We lay there together for hours. Although the waves of pain came and went, I had entered a calm, almost meditative state. My body was a ruinous mess, and both my dreams and the promises I had made to myself were broken, but I was content with Emmett by my side.

The next day I went to see an infectious disease specialist, who diagnosed me with amebiasis, resilient amoebic dysentery, which, in rare cases like mine, spreads to other organs. I was prescribed a robust combination of drugs, which offered a range of side effects that ironically mimicked the symptoms they would cure.

After two weeks of rest and much-needed cat therapy, with my physical strength returning, I felt I had the emotional gumption to swallow my pride and try to get my life back on track. So I did what I had told myself I would never do—I reached out to my old frat brothers.

Virtually all of them had settled in the city, and while I cringed thinking about the energy this postcollege ecosystem would generate, even that energy seemed preferable to what was starting to look like an eternity of isolation. And maybe living in the "real world" had changed them. So at Adam's insistence, I showed up to the next Saturday-night gathering at his apartment.

Adam, now an investment banker, wore fancier clothes and had a redder, thicker face, but he was the same soft-spoken, compassionate guy he had always been, and our chemistry felt as cathartic as ever.

Then Randy, Jesse, and Baum arrived. They collectively mocked my "Jesus shoe" Birkenstocks, and when I tried to jokingly respond with asking why they came dressed like their dads, they countered that I should never have come back from the Peace Corps and asked if being an unemployed, hairy, pretentious, faux-hemian nutbag was helping me meet more transvestites or extend the pipe dream of having a writing career. My blood boiled with familiar feelings of resentment and rage. Adam did his best to defuse the tension, but he was powerless against the force of the herd, who held more animosity toward me than I had anticipated. After taking almost forty-five minutes of abuse, I got up and left, adding yet another failed attempt to find a place for myself to my list.

Just as I was about to give up once and for all and succumb to my eternity of isolation, I ran into Dante's mother at my local grocery store. Though I hadn't seen or been in touch with him for years, he would love to get together, or so his mother said. This was as good a sign as any, so I dialed the number Dante's mom wrote down for me, and to my surprise, he invited me to meet him and some of his college friends at their favorite bar the next week.

I entered a nondescript sports bar, and there was Dante, much larger and much more muscular than I remembered, along with three of his friends, Santiago, Phil, and Dieter, all similarly coifed and all looking like they spent a remarkable amount of time at the gym. They seemed fascinated with my story, however, and asked me endless questions about my trip while drinking copious amounts of beer.

That fascination, in addition to the beer, gave me an instant buzz that lasted into even the more banal conversations touching on live music (mainly Phish), their jobs (all sales), the girls they were dating (multiple), and sports (both college *and* professional). With no knowledge and even less interest in any of these subjects, but touched by their acceptance, I sat contentedly, nodding in agreement and feeling like maybe I had found some humans I could tolerate and, more importantly, who could tolerate me.

When I got home that night, Emmett was waiting for me at the door, but as I began our therapeutic petting ritual, I felt something foreign behind one of his ears. When I examined the something in the light, I found a scaly gray growth. I became alarmed, and my mind flew to the worst-case scenario. Once again I had left Emmett to find something I felt was missing in my life, and now I would lose him, my only comfort, the only thing that still brought me joy.

My mother and I brought Emmett to the vet the next day. He took a biopsy, ran various tests, and finally, heartbreakingly, diagnosed Emmett with squamous cell carcinoma that an MRI revealed had spread into his internal organs. Euthanasia to save Emmett from the impending horrendous pain was the vet's recommendation. I flat-out refused, but within weeks, he had lost an alarming amount of weight, and his little body had begun to become brittle.

Watching his decline and his pain crushed me, and I began to shut down. Emmett could no longer hold food down, lost control of his bowels, and had trouble moving around, just as I had months before, and if I hadn't been so wrapped up in my own pain, maybe

I could have recognized his sooner. And so, to finally give Emmett the care he deserved from me and to return his steadfast love, I relented. We took him to the vet one last time, and he was put to rest. His body was cremated, and his ashes were placed in an urn that sat across from our couch on which I spent most of my waking hours, remembering that very first day he had walked into my life. The most important being, the kindest entity I had ever known, the deep soul who had gotten me through the toughest times of life was gone forever.

Chapter 8

Blur Time

HUMANS ARE A UNIQUE BLEND of nature—the genetic makeup we are born with—and nurture, the life experiences that form us. The randomness of that combination often prompted me to ponder if some coincidence or pure, blind luck could have shaped a dramatically different trajectory in my life. Perhaps if I had been born into a different family or were taught by another high school English teacher or sat next to a different stranger on the bus the last week, I could have been led in a direction that would have taken me to superhuman greatness instead of banal mediocrity.

And could that also have meant I had a suppressed potential still waiting to be realized? What if I never figured out how to tap into that potential? Was I living my life half asleep? Are the people who reach their full potential the only ones who really live, while the rest of us, pulled to conformity by social pressure, are just stuck "sheeple"?

These are the questions I bombarded myself with for as long as I can remember, and they came to represent the disparity between who I was and who I wanted to be. I was quiet, meek, frightened, tortured. But I wanted to be heroically impactful, incorruptible, fascinating, and bighearted—traits I found faintly in friends like Adam or acquaintances like the girl on the train in Morocco, but amply in the works of my cultural, philosophical, and literary idols. These two sides of me were in constant conflict, causing a cycle of self-torture.

Emmett's death changed all that. I wept for days, hyperventilating from the hysteria his dying unleashed. The connection between us soothed me in my times of greatest need. It was for me what a higher power is for believers. Like the promise of heaven in an afterlife, our bond promised there was good in the world and mitigated all the cruelty in which I wallowed. And when Emmett died, so did the part of me that always strove to be better, that felt pain for myself and others, that wanted the world to be a purer place. It was as if a button had been pushed to stop my compassion engine.

In its place sprouted a nihilistic numbness, which enveloped me like a chill and threatened to suffocate me. Rudderless and in too much pain to feel anything at all, I became an altogether different person, a shell. With no more North Star, no more security blanket, my capacity for feeling endlessly empathetic for the suffering of others, as I so often did, vanished.

I turned to Dante, Santiago, Philip, and Dieter to fill my weekends, sliding into the very mold I had once rejected. Our plans revolved around drinking and talking to women, and to my shock, I almost enjoyed the macho one-upmanship banter, which I had hated all my life. Even more surprisingly, I was able to tolerate their emphatic interest in sports, which I had always considered pointless games for the masses.

Back home, my parents' chagrin that I was unable to find a job was becoming insurmountable. Their biggest concern was my "lack of motivation," and they worried deferring my student loans and letting me live rent-free at home were enabling me. So I accepted a job referral from Phil for an entry-level position at a tech start-up in sales, a field I had previously pronounced to be the worst manifestation of humankind. It turns out that despite my reserved manner, I was a natural; I hit my quotas and even won a President's Club weekend vacation as a reward.

But not even that success could fill me up. With the guys' help, I turned to both weight training, a new distraction that kept my once-perpetual introspection dormant, and psychedelics, which Dante insisted would help me "tap into the muse" and maybe even spark inspiration for my writing.

That didn't happen. The drugs did, however, have the unintended effect of reawakening my existential crisis. Pain and regret mixed with yearning for creative expression were heightened by the crowds of people who swarmed the concerts I was dragged to with an almost religious intensity. We traveled to New Orleans for the Jazz & Heritage Festival and to California for Coachella. While everyone else seemed to enjoy the music, I reveled in the familiar feelings of torture and angst.

Despite all this, I continued to excel at my job—entirely on auto-pilot. I made deals and quickly rose up the corporate ladder of success. Now with an income, I moved out of my parents' place into a condo in trendy South Williamsburg, Brooklyn, but was too afflict-ed to appreciate the milestone. My world had turned into a hamster wheel of getting drunk, working out hungover, selling internet advertising space, going to music festivals, rinse and repeat. I was numbing myself. Time was a blur. I simply turned off whole parts of my personality, severely limiting my emotional range. More than anything I longed to have a substantive, authentic connection with another person, which could be a friend or an intimate relationship, which, given how much repressed pain I was in, was almost laugh-ably unrealistic. So I continued sleepwalking through life, put on a robot face, and just tried to get by, pitifully following everyone else around.

Eventually, there came a point when my friends found them-selves in committed relationships, and once again the odd man out, I was excluded from the coupled-up group activities. With no one to go out drinking with on the weekends or to take Molly with at concerts, I leaned into the only place my brain was finding pleasure those days—exercise.

What started out as a hobby—playing in a tennis league after work—gradually morphed into an obsession. I signed up for multiple leagues, filling my mornings, nights, and weekends with soccer practice, tennis matches, fencing classes, and CrossFit.

I had no other outlets, so I ramped up this schedule, learning new sports, joining more leagues, and pushing my body to an ever-greater extent. In addition to the pleasurable high my brain received, I hoped to make new friends or even meet a girl, but I was too awkward, too insecure, and too socially inept to make any inroads. The result: my existence consisted mostly of competing hard, not saying much, and keeping to myself.

The isolation didn't bother me, though; my new obsession filled what might have otherwise been a void. I got hooked on the adrenaline rush, and winning became everything to me. As numb, robotic, and bizarre as this existence was, I was satisfied with distracting myself from the pain of being alive.

Detached and high on exercise, with a self-imposed schedule of German efficiency, I moved through my life according to cuckoo clockwork. With no time for introspection, my brain disconnected from the melancholic demons that rise up from the bowels of human consciousness present in all of us, like mites that live in our eyelashes and bacteria in our stomachs.

Was this why everyone I knew stayed perpetually busy? Are we genetically programmed to foster meaning through activity, passion, religion, anything larger than ourselves so we don't default to the triviality of just being alive? Would we all just crumble if we didn't have something to believe in? Or was this just me and the aimless, vacant result of my fragility?

I didn't have definitive answers to these questions, until one day, a day like any other, I arrived at the gym at 5:30 a.m. to squeeze in a workout before volleyball practice. As team captain, this was pivotal to lead the team to victory in an upcoming tournament. But just before my second set of deadlifts, I made the mistake of turning my head, and therefore misaligning my spine, just as I lifted. That's a classic no-no, and as a result, I felt a pop at the lower part of my neck, then a series of bizarre sensations—a mixture of needle-like tingling and throbbing pain—streaked down my entire spine and into my left arm. In a state of panic and almost immobilized, I somehow managed to arrange a car service to take me home, where I laid on every ice pack I could find, then raided the freezer for bags of frozen food.

When I tried sitting up, jolts of violent pain forced me back down. I knew then that there would be no quick fix for this.

My tennis coach, who had worked with professional athletes, insisted I see a specialist, and I booked an appointment with a sports medicine neurologist, who slid me into his schedule the next day. After a lengthy examination plus an MRI, I was diagnosed with a herniated disc between the C5 and C6 vertebrae of my lower neck. The doctor explained that the pain, which was still excruciating, was a result of my body's swelling to protect itself. He then warned that if I continued my rigorous regiment, I would, in all likelihood, need to undergo spinal fusion surgery, which could be almost surely avoided by resting for up to two months.

This probably sounds reasonable to most people, but to me it was crippling. My mind roared thunderously. Sports were now the only things that released serotonin for me. I knew no other sources of pleasure. To be off the field and court and out of the gym, relegated to a sofa for two months, was simply my biggest nightmare at that point. What would keep the pain at bay now?

I pleaded with the specialist. Was there no in-office procedure, no traction machine, no injection that could speed up the process and give me my life back? But he only grew more steadfast, insisting that if I didn't follow his instructions, I would suffer irreparable damage, the kind that could irreversibly limit my mobility and wrap me in constant pain, and it would only become worse as I continued to age.

That worked. So out of fear and quivering with pain, I accepted my fate. I withdrew from every rec league and resigned myself to inactivity, the very thing I was avoiding at all costs. I would go back to being the boy who felt too much, the creator of my own self-imposed darkness. I felt doomed to suffer until the end of my time. And sadistic as it was, I felt a sense of comfort in the familiarity of this anguish.

It didn't take long for darkness to envelop me entirely. With nothing to occupy my mind, I became consumed with the questions that had haunted me since childhood. Why are we alive? Why is nature so cruel? What is the point of living? Why are people so selfish? Why do we bother to pretend that there is a meaning to the banal, arbitrary events, achievements, and relationships in our lives if we can die at any time and eventually cease to exist anyway? Caught in a pessimistic feedback loop of exploring the deep, dark dungeons of human consciousness, I found myself taking solace in resigning from life, in just giving up.

Although my neck began to heal from inactivity, my days passed in bed in a state of almost nonfunctioning autopilot. I occasionally futilely attempted to read a book or watch a movie, but my concentration was shot. I was able to summon just enough "normal" when my parents checked on me to reassure them I was fine. They saw through this, however, and staged an intervention in which they picked me up and escorted me to a hard-ass cognitive behavioral psychologist so I could undergo analysis for my melancholy.

As I unpacked the story of my life to a stranger, I learned I had an abnormally negative view of human beings, human nature, and the world. I exhibited an addictive personality as a way to escape from the underlying problems in my life. And most strangely but also most profound to me, I was suffering from a form of narcissistic personality disorder.

As far back as I could remember, I had always directed my time and energy internally, doing virtually nothing for anyone else, and this, the psychologist explained, was the source of my selfish, dark perspective. When this sank in, I saw my life in a new light. I really had never done anything at all for others. I could barely care for a plant. It was haunting, mind-boggling, disturbing, and—finally—enlightening.

Naturally, I thought of Emmett. I told the doctor about him and how much comfort and compassion our connection had provided me. An animal lover himself, he instantly grabbed onto this fondness for animals and suggested I could benefit greatly from having an animal companion in my life. Bright lights flashed in my brain, creating a warmth I hadn't felt in a long time. The glow instantly, if momentarily, made me forget my pain, which, up until that moment, had dwarfed everything else.

Now my thoughts were filled with sweet memories of Emmett's face, and I heard myself telling my psychologist I wanted to grow, to complete myself, to burst out of my comfort zone, to change. I would do so, I determined, by challenging myself. I would end my selfish streak and care for someone else.

I would become a dog dad.

Chapter 9

Rosenberg

EXCITED, SCARED, APPREHENSIVE, ANXIOUS, AND ecstatic beyond comprehension. These were some of the emotions that took turns fighting one another in my brain when I thought about taking on the responsibility of becoming a dog dad. The cells in my stomach knew it was the right thing for me, but what about the aforementioned innocent creature? While the carrot dangling in front of me pumped positive chemicals into my brain, the stick that followed was an aftertaste of primal fear. Weeks earlier I could barely get out of bed. What if I reverted to that, to scarcely being able to take care of *myself*? How would I be able to handle the responsibility of taking care of another living, breathing creature?

As with anything and everything people struggle with—and usually neglect to admit—my fear, once again, was based on failure. I had hit absolute rock bottom; if this didn't work out—if I failed at being a dog dad as I had failed at everything else—I wasn't sure I would have been able to handle such painful consequences one more time. I brought this up in a session with my cognitive psychologist, suggesting it as an excuse for delaying the proposed dog paternity, but my doctor pointed out that the delay tactic was the very crux of my narcissistic pathology. "Sack up," he told me as he suggested that, once and for all, I just break the mold and move on.

Reluctantly, I agreed.

Since I had no idea how the dog adoption process worked, nor was there anyone I could turn to, I did what seemed logical: I let the internet guide me. I googled the smartest dog breeds and picked two I recognized: poodles, which were hypoallergenic, and Australian shepherds, which had beautiful coat patterns and crazy-colored eyes. Without knowing much about either breed, I typed their names together and saw the keyword "Aussiedoodle," the crossbreed of the two. This led me to an image search for Aussiedoodle puppies—tiny, surprised, and embarrassed guinea-pig faces exuding a sweet, awkward innocence that would melt Satan's heart.

In my naivete, I clicked at random on one marked available, which brought me to the website of a Michigan-based family breeder—that is, someone who breeds and raises dogs for a family rather than a commercial puppy mill dealing with pet shops. The website listed a number to call, so I obliged. After waiting for five minutes and almost giving up, the phone was answered by an older woman. Right off the bat, she began explaining why Aussiedoodles were the most loyal and intelligent breed the world had ever known; within minutes, despite also hearing about her favorite scripture passages, her kids and grandkids, and her various ailments, she had me completely convinced.

Unfortunately, the pup whose picture had I asked about was already spoken for, but she suggested an alternative. While almost all the littermates of the puppy in the photo had been adopted, there was one exception—a male with a birth defect in whom no one seemed interested. Since I had always thought of myself in just this way—born with a defect—it was all I needed to hear. I did not need to see a picture or hear another word. "I want that puppy," I told her. Fate had spoken.

In that case, she told me, the only cost would be the dog's transportation, which she would arrange by plane to JFK. She assured me not to be concerned because "I regularly ship dogs to the East Coast." I thought this sounded strange, but I was so overcome with excitement and anxiety that I simply took her word for it.

"Do you have a name in mind?" she asked before we got off the phone. I was just about to tell her I hadn't when, looking out my window in South Williamsburg, Brooklyn, I saw a Hasidic family walking across the street—a common occurrence in that neighborhood. So I told her that to make the dog feel comfortable and fit into our neighborhood, and to honor my father's family history, "I'm going to call him Rosenberg."

I spent the week that followed researching, ordering supplies, and counting down every second. Then I headed for the airport, accompanied by an electrifyingly frantic level of excitement and by a stomach twitching with a mixture of intimidation and anticipation.

I went to the wrong gate, then to the wrong station, then finally to the receiving area that accepts animal cargo, where I learned Rosenberg's flight was delayed. I waited for hours until finally a small crate rolled in, and the uniformed baggage handler a few feet from me called my name.

I signed for the crate, picked it up, walked twenty feet, then placed it on the linoleum floor to look inside. What I saw was the frightened face of a baby brown bear. The face had peeked out to see where it was, then darted back, frightened by the chaotic world it had just endured. My heart dropped as I realized how overwhelmed he must be, and I began to consider the terrible trauma of delays, turbulence, cold temperatures, and industrial sounds this small, soft baby must have suffered through during the long flight. Bags of bricks hit me in the face: this was all my fault! I would never forgive myself for—yet again!—being so irresponsibly selfish and stupid. There were tears in my eyes as I opened the crate, ushered him out, then held him in my arms as he meekly looked around, panting, as bewildered as I.

His tiny body and bones felt jellylike, and his coat of coarse, high-static brown hair stood up straight in thousands of awkward angles. His feet smelled of urine from the long trip, but it was overpowered by the sweetest puppy smell, a combination of vanilla and freshly cut hay. His body moved in the erratic motions of an animated film, probably because he had no doubt been hyperventilating from the new sights and sounds of the trip, the infinite largeness of the world. As he lay in my lap, he clutched at me, clawing my torso with his little nails and staring at me with big, human eyes full of panic and pure innocence that made him seem more human than humans themselves.

Instinctively, I began massaging his head and whispering to him. He was panting so hard I could feel his heart's beating thumps wherever my hand touched his body. I was afraid it might stop. Somewhere in the periphery of my vision, I noticed a crowd of people watching him too, but I paid them no attention. I just kept massaging him, softly repeating, "Rosenberg, I am your daddy now. I know this is hard, but I love you, and I promise everything will be okay. I promise you everything will be okay."

By the time we arrived at my apartment, my nerves were in overdrive. Rosenberg had not calmed down even an iota, so I was holding him as gently as I could in one arm while grasping his empty crate with the other. I had laid out all the supplies ahead of time so everything awaiting him would be just right: organic treats, wee-wee pads, chew toys, and puppy brain-development games. The second we walked in, he relieved himself on a pad, sniffed a few treats, then turned around, seemingly in disgust, ignoring everything else.

Knowing he had to eat, I located a bag of kibble in his crate, put it in a bowl, and set it down—whereupon he lunged at it ravenously. His hunger abated, he apprehensively began to pussyfoot around the apartment, smelling and nudging the rug, the garbage can, the sofa. I gave him space to do so but followed him, nervous my puppy-proofing efforts may have missed something and my failure could result in him hurting himself.

A few minutes later, he was gone…disappeared into thin air.

I searched every inch of the premises, only to find him back in his crate.

I sat down on the floor next to the crate and tried to lure him out with squeak toys and treats at the edge of the door. Nothing worked. He was still panting loudly, seemingly out of panic, and would not budge. There was no other option; I sat and waited.

And waited.

After some twenty minutes, his head emerged, slowly, from the crate. Then his tiny body followed, and he turned to see me staring at him. His head cocked sideways as if he were asking what I was doing there or as if he expected me to ask him that very question. As an answer, I offered him my hand to smell, which he did. Then I scooped his body up slowly, carried him to the couch, and sat the two of us down. I heard his heart race again and his panting increase, feeding our combined anxieties. As this sped up, I began to sweat, and my stomach seemed to pulsate as I realized what a monster I was for putting him on that flight alone and wrenching him away from everything and everyone he had ever known. I was the reason for a trauma causing him irreparable damage and suffering—a crime for which there could be no forgiveness.

Naturally, this sent me into the unmistakable early stages of a panic attack, so I quickly caught my breath and began to breathe deeper. I picked Rosenberg up again, placed him on my stomach, and began stroking his head and body in long, patterned motions in an attempt to soothe us both. We lay there together in just that way for more than an hour until I felt his body finally give up his fear and start to calm down. Then, in what seemed like an instant, he fell asleep.

I didn't move. Not one millimeter. I just stared at his little angelic torso, studying everything about him. His butter-soft ears; his small, furry paws with alternating black and brown fingernails; his sharp baby teeth; his defined, crisp white whiskers; his wet button nose. He was *tiny*, weighing in at six pounds at most, and the generous amount of fuzzy hair on the top of his back made him look even more awkwardly adorable.

I continued to lie there in silence, not moving a muscle and marveling at the existence of this sleeping, living, breathing, wild baby teddy bear. I just kept staring, completely hypnotized by his presence.

And that's when I realized I had not been thinking about or obsessing over my problems or the never-ending list of things I found wrong with my life and myself.

It was a revelation. I now knew my life had to be dedicated to doing everything humanly possible to bring happiness to this pure soul who, like Emmett before him, channeled all the benevolence and wholesomeness present in the world. I now understood, with searing clarity, that so long as this puppy existed, he provided me with undeniable living proof that despite all the unfairness and misery in the world, there was good too. And I vowed that from that day forward, my needs would be subservient to his, and I would always do anything, no matter what, to make him happy. The entire weight of my world depended on it.

So I began, through trial and error, proximity, and osmosis, to study his habits and understand his needs. I identified his anxiety triggers—easy, since his face could not hide his vulnerability and fear—so I could make sure they were avoided and we could strengthen his self-esteem and build up his confidence. Outdoors, he was deathly afraid of car horns and other loud noises, but his archnemeses were the satanic plastic bags or any other gravity-defying, poltergeist-like object carried by the wind. Indoors, he was afraid of windows and preferred to curl up under furniture or to lie down in hallways. He also needed to be in sight of me at all times; if not, as I learned, he would scratch the paint off the side of the bathroom door. This, of course, meant I would never have any privacy ever again, which, for a person who could barely take care of myself, was both bloodcurdling and faintly cathartic.

He drank more water when it was filtered and extra cold—back-of-the-fridge cold. His relationship to food was more catlike than doglike. While at first he had seemed to devour everything in front of him, after discovering better options, he rejected anything not up to snuff. After only a week, he went from scarfing down kibble to spurning it totally. He also rebuffed a multitude of gourmet organic treats, with the exception of one—the most expensive one. I had to present him with multiple meal options before I discovered his preference for organic chicken, well-done, off the bone, served at room temperature, and cut into small pieces. And at a certain anxiety level or in certain moods, he would only eat the chicken if it was hand-fed. I loved it.

Once we squared away food, I went to work on the cornerstone of the human-canine interspecies relationship—the walk, which was also the only exercise I could do with my healing herniated disc. Because I was so used to seeing humans and dogs walk together, I had assumed it was an instinct that came naturally to both. I quickly learned that was not the case. Without any experience on a lead, puppies have no idea how to walk with humans—and vice versa—producing one of the clumsiest scenes imaginable.

Rosenberg's aversion to loud sounds prompted me to find elaborate routes that minimized street noise, debris, and foot traffic, all of which could trigger his flight response and force me to pick him up right away. It took countless hours of practice and awkward fumbling until he—and I—felt comfortable, and it manifested itself in his mastery of the Poodle Strut, that unique swagger that epitomizes poodle arrogance. Rosenberg had no arrogance, though; his Australian shepherd side saw to that. But the slight butt-shake in his stride, the sass, was definitely inherited from his poodle side, and this tiny bit of extra confidence marked a turning point in him.

I made sure to greet this achievement with applause, petting, and verbal encouragement, all of which put a smile on his face that stretched from ear to ear—like a human—upping his confidence even more. As we continued our walks in perfect stride, his sass took hold, and an immense wave of pride washed over me, as I knew my efforts were working.

Devoting my time, thoughts, and energy away from myself and onto something—someone—else generated a feeling of satisfaction I had not experienced before. Not only had I forgotten my failures, my self-professed lack of meaning, and my social anxiety, but things were also beginning to make sense in my brain—things like the context of my life and possibly even the world.

Chapter 10

Building Blocks

IN MY NEVER-ENDING QUEST TO find respite from my demons, I had read countless self-help books by experts in philosophy, theology, and psychology. Each book claimed to offer its own foolproof path to achieving a natural state of happiness. No matter how many times I reread each book, though, I couldn't find any practical takeaways. The lack of effectiveness wasn't a failure of merit on the part of the self-help authors, but rather of my state of mind, which can be best understood by the quote, "To a man with a hammer, everything looks like a nail." That is to say that like so many others who suffer from the sad sickness that afflicted me, I was so consumed by my own suffering and search for meaning that I wasn't capable of experiencing anything else.

I was trapped, stuck in my obsessively self-centered, narcissistic fortress. I had built the walls up so high that they created a self-fulfilling prophecy: I simply could not see outside, much less find a way out.

So the moment when I officially flipped my attention away from my own needs and focused solely on Rosenberg's, I found space for empathy, which snapped me out of my dysfunctional, purgatorial pity party. I now had a mission—call it a religion: a reason to get up in the morning, get out and exercise, even socialize. I was now governed by a force a hundred times stronger than gravity. Nothing on earth could stop me from taking care of my puppy; nothing could keep me from giving him the best life humanly possible.

I researched it, digging deep into how to be a great dog dad, and I learned how critically important it is to socialize puppies right after their first round of vaccinations. Like baby humans, puppies go through an "imprinting stage," during which everything they are exposed to will be engraved in their puppy brains, determining how they adapt, build tolerance, and learn the behavioral rules that will shape their compatibility with the world for the rest of their lives.

I quickly found a twice-weekly puppy class in my neighborhood, attended by furry students of all different breeds, shapes, sizes, colors, and—most importantly—dispositions. There we met Moses, a baby basset hound; Henri, a three-month-old springer spaniel; Murray, a still-tiny Great Dane; Bartholomew, a floppy golden retriever; and Pippa, a rotund and gluttonous Pugalier—that is, a mix of pug and Cavalier King Charles spaniel. Despite their adorable differences, they were all awkwardly new to the world, clumsily still learning how to interact with one another.

The class began with a few bonding exercises between pup and parent followed by free play, when all the puppies got to meet and interact. Everyone else's puppy was quick to smell, play, and run around with the others, but Rosenberg was instantly intimidated, and he retreated, hiding behind me, panting hard, seemingly overwhelmed with anxiety.

The masterfully perceptive puppy teacher sensed Rosenberg's trepidation at once and told me he had what is called a selective disposition. It was important, the teacher said, to let him go at his own pace. And after a few minutes, just as the teacher predicted, Rosenberg slowly poked his little head out from behind my legs, crept toward the group, then cautiously began to smell the baby basset hound's butt—an "introduction" that Moses returned in kind. Rosenberg seemed to gain confidence from this exchange, and he began to walk around the room, greeting each puppy he saw.

The other puppy parents in the class took notice of Rosenberg's friendliness and began to form a crowd around him and turn their attention on me. At first this of course made me feel self-conscious, but as they started asking questions about Rosenberg, and as we all began comparing our dogs' personalities and our dog-parent rituals, care tactics, and potty-training progress, I began to feel more comfortable. Pretty soon, Andrew, dad of baby golden retriever Bartholomew; Thaddeus, dad of baby Great Dane Murray; Brandon, dad of baby Pugalier Pippa; and I had all exchanged phone numbers and talked about arranging our own extracurricular puppy playdates.

As we chatted, my gaze was continually pulled to Rosenberg. He was still in a butt-sniffing frenzy, but there was a big smile on his little face, and as we locked eyes, he registered his approval of all these goings-on. In fact, toward the end of the free-play session, he began prancing around the room in a joyous exhibition of energy and ecstasy. Witnessing his delight brought me to that feeling my various self-help books called a natural state of happiness. Remarkably, my interactions with these other dog dads felt light. I wasn't nervous about what I would say or how I would come off. I didn't feel self-conscious or wonder if any of them liked me. Even though I wasn't used to anything remotely like it, everything felt natural, peaceful, even normal.

Watching Rosenberg thrive in puppy school solidified for me that his confidence was increasing exponentially, making mincemeat of his initial paralyzing anxiety, and some portion of his new self-assurance spilled over onto me. Whenever he learned a new command, socialized with another dog, or overcame a fear, I would applaud and give him a treat, and since the world was still so new to him, every day seemed like the best day of his life. Witnessing the ecstatic more-human-than-human expressions on his face filled me with pride, both in how far he had come and in how I had helped him get there.

We continued attending the puppy classes, Rosenberg continued developing friendships with the other pups, and I continued growing friendships with their parents and interacting with the people in my neighborhood in a way I'd never done before. On our daily walks, which could total as much as ten miles along the same route at about the same times each day, we encountered many of the same people, all of whom smiled the moment they laid eyes on Rosenberg's precious face. Seeing people smiling at my dog immediately constituted a positive association in my mind and instinctively caused me to smile back. Astonishingly, I seemed to be developing a friendly, welcoming, even inviting disposition.

One morning we passed a hip-looking mother and her daughter of about six or seven, who locked eyes with Rosenberg and stopped dead in her tracks. This was, by now, a typical occurrence, but what the little girl said next stopped *me* in my tracks. She looked at Rosenberg, then looked at me, and with a child's bluntness, said, "Mom, he looks just like his puppy!"

The mortified mother shushed her daughter at once, then apologized profusely. I assured them both it was the greatest compliment anyone could ever give me.

"It makes sense," I told the little girl. "Since I *am* his dad, we *should* look alike."

When I told this story at the next puppy class, however, I was surprised to find out that everyone, including the teacher, had been thinking the same thing, had been marveling over this crazy coincidence behind my back.

Hans, the dad to baby basset hound Moses, took it a step further. He worked in fashion and thought Rosenberg and I should dress alike, men's clothing for me and kids' sizes for my dog. Naturally, I assumed Hans was joking, so I agreed and laughed it off. To my surprise, though, he showed up to the next class with matching outfits, insisting I promise to wear them in public and report back.

It was one of those bizarre things where, almost overnight, everywhere I went, strangers on the street stopped us to tell me how much they thought I looked like my pup. Although flattered, I wasn't always comfortable with the attention. Some days it made me feel special and proud; other times I had a suspicion people were ogling us as if we were freaks, pointing and laughing at our expense.

Despite my mercurial feelings, however, I knew I had to follow through on my promise to Hans and wear his gift in public; it would eat at me forever if I didn't. By the next class, I knew it was time for me to set a date and get it done.

That Sunday morning, Rosenberg and I went to Prospect Park for the weekly off-leash dog run. For those who have never seen this beautiful sight, it takes place on what is effectively a massive, picturesque grassy meadow, with every dog breed imaginable frolicking, fetching, and living their best lives. After Rosenberg had an hour of play and had drunk plenty of water, we walked a little way to an adjacent section of the park where I dressed him in his matching clothes.

A few seconds later, a group of some fifteen children, all holding hands, all under the watchful eyes of their chaperones, approached our little piece of the park. One of the kids locked eyes with me, pointed at us, and yelled, "He's dressed like his doggy!" The other kids stopped and stared, and suddenly the entire group, children and adults, had surrounded us.

It was a chain reaction—dominoes falling every which way. One kid after another pointed, laughed, shouted. Their little bodies jumped up and down like machines, and the looks on their faces were priceless. They were downright jubilant. And their jubilation made more people take notice, until suddenly there was a crowd of at least twenty-five people around Rosenberg and me.

It felt surreal—like it was happening in slow motion. I had always felt intimidated when any attention had come my way, but this was distinctly different. I felt a rush of chemicals I wasn't familiar with gushing through my brain. Every synapse was overloaded with bliss, and being the cause of pleasure to these people sent me higher than I had ever been, a high that dwarfed all the lows I had ever had—combined. I felt electrified, as if a revolution had occurred in my consciousness. A switch had been turned in my brain. Thoughts burst out faster than I could comprehend them, but the through line was unambiguous: putting my love, my sense of responsibility, and my energy into Rosenberg had knocked down my walls, unblocked whatever had sent me into my darkness, and set me on the road to happiness. The love, the accountability, and the constant companionship I had gained as a dog dad had changed me. After years in the same rut, I felt I was finally entering a new chapter of my life—something I never thought could or would happen.

Suddenly, I had a mission in life.

The way I saw it, if I could be blessed with the gift of looking almost identical to the being who had saved me, and if that was something that could make other people happy—make them smile, make them laugh—then I had a responsibility to pay it back. I had an obligation to spread that happiness—that help—to as many other people as possible.

So that very day, I committed myself to do just that. I vowed to help others overcome their sad sickness. That was my real reason for being alive, and it seemed to me like a good one.

Chapter 11

The Dog Styler

THERE ARE TIMES IN OUR lives that mark a monumental
change—a radical shift or divergence onto a wholly different path.
From that instant, everything is different. Movies like to show us
this moment, dramatizing it as an epiphany that stops the hero mid-
conversation, eyes aglow, as movie magic—enhanced lighting, color
saturation, and a new wardrobe—takes over. In real life, however,
when these seismic life shifts occur, there's no director to stage it,
no lighting technician to illuminate it, no soundtrack to amplify it.
We are often way too close to the storyline to even realize it as it is
happening to us, to grasp its significance, to understand that our
lives have fundamentally changed forever.

My realization that I could make people happy by simply being
with Rosenberg was such a change, but I didn't comprehend the
weight of it just then. It was only later that I realized how different
I had felt. My thoughts became clearer, I had double the energy,
and instead of obsessing about the meaninglessness of life because

everyone will eventually die, everything suddenly and inexplicably seemed to have a silver lining.

While I couldn't comprehend the gravity of the change, I did feel a tug—more like a magnetic force—that a change was happening. I had no idea what path or form it would take, but I knew it was much bigger, stronger, and more important than I was, and I knew it was something I had never felt before in my life: the desire to spread positivity and help others. Just based on how much my emotional health had improved through Rosenberg's love, not to mention through the reaction of people who saw us dressed alike, I knew in my bones I was armed with everything I needed to make a monumental impact on the world. The only problem was that I still didn't know how.

Luckily, I was now an active member of a new friend group—the dog-parent friend group. I also knew that with their help, I would find a solution.

At the start of the next and last puppy class—the graduation ceremony—I relayed what had happened in Prospect Park, giving full credit to Hans, and explained how it led to my new mission in life. After the class, a group of us headed over to Lucky Dog, a dog-themed and therefore friendly bar a few blocks away. Over drinks we obsessed over the hilarious personalities of our furry kids and talked about the curative impact they were having on our lives. Someone in the group pulled up a photo for reference, then showed us the dog's Instagram account. I had heard of Instagram but knew little about it, but when I realized dogs could have profiles that could reach thousands of people, I thought this sounded like the perfect way to spread my new message with Rosenberg. I could post pictures of us dressing alike and receive the same attention I had in the park. But there were some big hurdles. Among them: I barely knew how to use a camera and knew even less about social media. I told the group as much and did something I had never done before—I admitted I needed help *and* asked for it. Hans, ever the angel, suggested I contact @thedogstyler, a Brooklyn-based photographer he knew from the fashion world who now exclusively photographed fashionable dogs.

That night, after cooking and hand-feeding Rosenberg small bites of his cage-free, humanely treated organic chicken, I studied @thedogstyler's work and read every word of every article that had been written about her. Originally from New Jersey, she was a street-style photographer who became disenchanted with the fashion world and, in reaction to its snobbery, pivoted into something that would combine her obsession with couture and her passion for dogs. Her work involved intricate set designs and contrasts of colors as she combined the William Wegman–like anthropomorphizing of dogs with the fantastical visuals of *Alice in Wonderland*. This work—and the fact that someone this cool actually existed—blew my mind, inspiring the rapid creation of my own Instagram account through which I messaged her my life story. My hope was nothing less than to spark her interest in our potential collaboration.

I checked my account more than fifty times that night and again the next day, but there was no reply. I saw no other option but to message her again—twice more, in fact. I then realized I might be coming off as both desperate and aggressive, so I deleted my account entirely to save face and erase any evidence. I spent the next few days kicking myself for blowing what could have been my best and only opportunity, then formulated a new plan: I would pitch her in person.

From her photos I learned she lived in Williamsburg, as I did, and that she frequented McCarren Park, home of the neighborhood's biggest and best gathering spot for dogs. Going there was also the logical next step for Rosenberg's exercise and social development, so with the prospect of killing three birds with one stone, we started going there every day.

After twenty-one days in a row, however, the Dog Styler was still nowhere to be found. Fortunately, Rosenberg loved the park and made a few more dog friends, so it still seemed worthwhile despite having to give up on any collaboration with this amazingly creative woman.

But on day twenty-two, as Rosenberg and I were in the middle of a game of tennis ball fetch, a woman holding a camera walked into the dog park. She was tall with huge anime eyes and wore silver high-top sneakers and a peacock-bright wrap dress that could be seen a mile away. My heart began racing, my stomach began twitching, and the palms of my hands broke out into a sweat.

In awe and intimidated, I did everything I could to play it cool—I casually threw the ball at her so Rosenberg had to run to her. Serendipitously, he stopped in front of her and locked eyes with a King

Charles spaniel she was petting. The two dogs began sniffing each other, and she extended her hand to Rosenberg, who, despite habitually exhibiting trepidation around new people, moved closer, close enough to start licking the fingers of her right hand.

I could barely believe it, but with the pit of my stomach in a knot and my head feeling like a balloon pumped with adrenaline, I approached them. My voice cracked, and I heard myself stutter slightly as I introduced myself and told her I was a big fan of her work.

She seemed perplexed. Her beautiful face shifted from smiling to bewildered as she apologized, then asked me to repeat what I had said. I tried again, louder and, I hoped, clearer.

"Thanks," she said, smiling sheepishly but still kneeling and petting Rosenberg.

There was a pause. Then she stood up, extended her hand, and said, "I'm Chantal. Nice to meet you."

An uncomfortable silence followed before I managed to introduce Rosenberg, then myself—again. I started to ask if she would consider photographing us, but she interrupted to say she was looking for "adorable dogs like Rosenberg" and their dads for an upcoming Father's Day assignment for the *Huffington Post*.

"I think you'd be perfect for it," she said.

We exchanged numbers, set a date for the next Saturday, and went our separate ways. Walking home from the park, I felt high as a kite, higher maybe than I ever had before, like I was hit by a tsunami, an earthquake, and a landslide all at once.

From that moment on, all I could think about was seeing her again. Everything about her—her vintage style, her passion for her work, her kind face—exuded an inhibition-free expression of self, the kind of person I never was but always wanted to be. With so much at stake, I couldn't let our next interaction go wrong, so I wrote and rewrote my follow-up texts, seeking to confirm the logistics for our shoot and asking for a midweek call to discuss the creative concept. Then I went to work brainstorming and writing on Post-it notes—which I then stuck to my walls so I could reference if need be—topics we could discuss in the hopes of minimizing any awkward silences and alleviating my fear of being boring. Thinking about it more, though, I worried the Post-it note operation would lead me to change conversation topics too abruptly, which would be even more awkward, so I scrapped it altogether and came up with a new fail-safe: talking about 3D printing, which was all the rage at the time. It didn't matter that I had little comprehension of it, because no one I knew did, so I assumed she wouldn't either and would thus be impressed by my knowledge.

After all the anticipation, when we did in fact speak over the phone, everything flew out the window. She was comforting, calm, vulnerable, and did something I wasn't used to—she asked me questions about myself. Feeling at ease, I told her the truth—how Rosenberg had come into my life at one of my lowest points and had saved me. I explained how his companionship and unconditional love had taught me that the secret of contentment was caring for and helping other people, which I had never known until now. I shared how my experience with Rosenberg had unlocked my need to spread the limitless potential of the healing powers of dogs. I blathered on and on—until, with apologies, she interrupted me.

She told me she had lost her father to brain cancer when she just turned twelve, and her mother, to help her two daughters cope with the trauma of this tragedy, had given in and presented them with what they had long coveted—a white toy poodle named Cocoa. Into the void that could never be filled pranced the dog she referred to as her love battery, distracting the sisters from their pain, healing their hearts, and becoming the connective tissue that brought her family together again and kept it whole.

My eyes welled with tears as I listened to her story, Rosenberg on my lap listening too. I knew I couldn't begin to understand what it must have felt like to lose a parent, and this put the suffering I had experienced through relentless self-obsession into a fresh context. It couldn't be clearer that Chantal knew so much more about life and about the magical healing powers of animals than I could possibly fathom. At that moment I felt a connection with her, the deepest I had ever felt with anyone in my entire life.

She told me how she had always gotten along better with dogs than with people and how she became a dog fashion photographer, carving out her own niche and lifting people's spirits as Cocoa had done for her and her family. Everything she told me sounded mind-bogglingly analogous to my own life, and waves of excitement I had never felt before ran through every part of my body. As someone who perpetually felt overlooked and eternally unlucky, there was a moment when I thought I was being had by a cosmic joke. But no. This was reality. *She* was reality, and my brain lit up at the serendipity of finding someone so genuine, kind, gifted, and beautiful, who understood my life's calling even better than I did. It was as improbable as lightning striking in the same spot twice. And it upended everything. That there could be someone like her, who loved dogs and felt the same way about their healing potential as I did, transformed my long-held beliefs about the inherent cruelty of nature and the harsh realities of life—and effectively forced me to give up the grudges I held against the world.

That night as I lay awake in bed, with Rosenberg passed out at my feet, too wired to sleep, my brain churned through the waves of ideas, epiphanies, and feelings of euphoria crashing in my head. I did my best to try to analyze and make sense of it all, but my thoughts were racing, overlapping one another, fighting for dominance and brain space.

After hours of deep breathing and petting Rosenberg, I came to one monumental conclusion: I was in love with Chantal. Even though I barely knew her, I felt as if we had known each other for years, which was all the stranger because for so long, I hardly knew—or more accurately, *understood*—my own feelings, let alone myself. What was so revolutionary for me, something that might be taken for granted by everyone else, was that I was actually *feeling*, and feeling positive emotions at that. I was connecting with another person emotionally, something I now realized I hadn't really ever done before. As clichéd as it sounds, it was as if a spell was lifted, and the real me, the person I had always dreamed of being, was coming to life.

With this understanding, I knew that if Chantal would have me, I would have her—as a friend, a creative collaborator, a pen pal, an acquaintance, whatever—until the day I died. No matter the connection, it would be enough for me. I was pulled toward her in a way that felt stronger and more glorious than I'd ever felt before. I just needed to be in her orbit.

I started this chapter by noting that while seismic life shifts are often undetectable while they're happening, there are also times when they smack you like a ton of bricks. They happen in slow motion and are so imprinted on your senses that, even years later, a scent or a song can bring you right back to that very moment, can recreate those very sensations. This was what that phone call with Chantal was for me.

But I do have to give credit where credit is due: Rosenberg's companionship and unconditional love had enabled me to build self-esteem, discover my passion, and lay the groundwork to be in this position in the first place—to be able to *feel*.

That is the milestone marked by that phone call, and I knew I would never, ever take it for granted.

Chapter 12

Cahoots

"WHEN THE RIGHT PERSON COMES along, you'll just know it." "Be patient; everything happens for a reason." "It'll happen when you least expect it." These phrases are often said by married people, couples, or those who seem older and wiser to those who are struggling excruciatingly to find a partner. Frustratingly, these annoying, patronizing clichés end up being dead true, and when something is right—whether a relationship, profession, or broader life decision—it will feel natural and everything will fall into place. Cynics will say this is because of luck, happenstance, or a predetermined "fate." But those patronizers know we are all governed by the inevitability of time, and with time comes opportunities, connections, and experiences that can lead to life-altering new chapters wherein everything we knew, or thought we knew, will be transformed and incomprehensibly turned around.

My first shoot with Chantal will be forever immortalized in my memory as one of those opportunities. It happened the following

Saturday in Central Park. To celebrate summer, Chantal dressed Rosenberg and me in matching seersucker suits with purple bow ties. Then she framed us with lush greenery "to pull out the green from our hypnotically matching eyes." Not knowing what to expect, Rosenberg and I were both nervous, but Chantal was simultaneously professional and laid-back, putting us at ease, so apart from wearing suits in the blistering heat, everything was peachy. I was enchanted watching her work. She knew exactly what to say and do; she made it look effortless. Nothing—even people getting in our way, throwing snide comments, or giving us dirty looks—bothered her. She let it roll off her, like a duck dunked in water. She was perpetually lighthearted, almost airy, the complete opposite of and perfect complement to the exhausting complexity of me.

What warmed my heart most was how patient she was with Rosenberg and how concerned she was about his comfort; she had even brought along a mini electric fan to cool him off between takes. When we weren't shooting, he hovered as close to Chantal as he could, doing his best to lick the sweat off her legs—a further testament to me of her divinity.

The image of us she ultimately chose became the lead of her *Huffington Post* dog dad Father's Day article, which ended up going viral, igniting thousands of shares and comments from people obsessing about the uncanny likeness between Rosenberg and me, asking to know more about us, and begging Chantal to photograph us more. While this was the exact outcome I desired, I felt embarrassed by it. I still do. To this day—as I tap the keys on my keyboard this very moment—just writing about successes like this makes me cringe as if I were dragging my nails across a chalkboard.

But the public had spoken, Chantal's and my values were aligned, and now our chemistry in working together was established. So after much persistence, Chantal agreed "in theory" to become my partner—the photographer, stylist, and creative director of my soon-to-be-launched Topher Brophy Instagram account. Our broad-strokes mission was clear: to spread the life-changing love we experienced through animal companionship to others to help ease suffering and make the world a better place. What we still had to figure out were the details, so we set up a date for the following week, agreeing that she would come to my apartment.

The mere thought of her coming over generated an insurmountable amount of positive anxiety that sent tingles up and down my spine. The moment she came through the door, Rosenberg barked loudly, then greeted her in happy hysteria with excitable, endless licks, interrupted only by a few extra-high-pitched squeals that had previously been reserved solely for me. Chantal wore shoes with rainbow-striped heels, a purple-and-yellow silk hair wrap, and a frilly white Victorian-inspired dress. When she gave me a hello kiss on the cheek, I inhaled her perfume, jasmine mixed with sandalwood, and my heart pounded even faster.

I quickly offered her a seat, which she thanked me for, then ignored. Instead, she walked around my living room, assessing the lighting and concluding that given the high ceilings, we could transform this space into our photography studio, which would be ultra-convenient since I lived alone and she had two roommates. With that established, we dove in.

I felt incredibly lucky that her strengths filled the gaps that were my weaknesses. As a photographer and stylist who knew how to sew her own clothes, coordinate colors, draw, and apply makeup, she would lead the way on everything visual; in those realms, she was obviously the expert. I had little to no experience, interest, or talent in those arenas, and I had never encountered anyone who was as gifted in them as she clearly was.

Because I still dreamed of being a writer, and because I was perpetually introspective and obsessed with mankind's enduring existential crisis, I would handle all the messaging and writing. Having just recovered from the darkest depths of emotional purgatory, I could relate easily to others who felt helpless. I felt that put me in a prime position to get through to them and, hopefully, by sharing what I'd learned, bring them the help they sought.

Launching the account, we decided, would be a three-step process. First, get people to look. Easy—Chantal's art direction and Rosenberg's and my striking resemblance had that covered. Then, get people to laugh. We needed to incorporate humor and surrealism into our posts to acknowledge the absurdity of our existence and help us to cope with the paradox of knowing we will all die. As I continued to heal and grow increasingly more comfortable in my own skin, I grew more and more inclined to act as a jester, not a moper, and was surprised at how easily this came to me. And finally—we hoped—get people to listen. I understood that to get the message across, I would need to embrace my newly realized emotions, and if I were going to pull on the heartstrings of people at the receiving end of the message, I would also need to combine real sentiment with brutal honesty. But first I needed to do a deep dive into the platform.

Until then I had not had much exposure to or interest in social media, so I plunged into the online world. It seemed about 95 percent of everything happening on social media was either narcissistic grandstanding or a way for people to project an inauthentic image of themselves—an image free of the problems, flaws, and anxieties everyone else in the world lived with on a daily basis. It was a raging one-upmanship, a contest to determine who was the least flawed—and therefore the least "human" human on earth. It all struck me as a Cold War arms race, and the weapons people were racing to acquire—likes and followers—were based on lies, pure and simple. But the blatant inauthenticity people were firing into the online universe was, in fact, a dead giveaway for what they were truly feeling: fear that they weren't attractive enough or wealthy enough or woke enough and fear of missing out on what everybody else was so obviously enjoying and thriving on.

To me social media at best offered harmless, meaningless brain candy; at worst, it epitomized the excess and decline of Western civilization and earmarked humanity's descent into a lower level of evolution.

Given my feelings on the subject—with which Chantal basically agreed—our foray into social media would be the complete opposite. Our main tenet, after all, was to help make the world a better place, and falling into an algorithmic pattern of unhealthy groupthink would only add to the piling-on of other people's unhappiness, another downward step in humanity's decline. So we established that, whenever possible, no matter how sugary the photograph, we would relate it to subjects that actually mattered. We were not going to be another cheap-shot, cute-photos-of-puppies platform. We had a purpose, a mission—to show how dogs can make us better humans and can help us heal ourselves and maybe even the world. We would maintain authenticity by talking openly and straightforwardly about my pain, and we would tell the story of my transformation, enabled by Rosenberg's love, and how it led to my personal goal of being the ultimate dog dad.

Finally, we agreed that because our goal wasn't to make money, if we were fortunate enough to generate demand for what we were "selling," we would dedicate as much work as possible to promoting charities that helped animals, researched cures for diseases, championed the underrepresented, and helped children in need. We vowed never to allow ourselves to stray from this.

With these tenets in place, we moved into the next stage: generating ideas, finding inspiration for our work, and, most exciting for me, spending more time together. With Rosenberg at our side at all times, we went to museums, flea markets, and art exhibits. We researched historical figures from Alexander the Great, who named a city in India after his dog, Peritas, to Tokugawa Tsunayoshi, the Japanese shogun who was obsessed with and instituted protection laws for dogs, to Franklin D. Roosevelt, whose dog, Fala, was so loved he's the only presidential pet to be immortalized in statue next to his human, to Paul McCartney, whose English sheepdog, Martha, is the subject of the Beatles' song "Martha My Dear." All the while, Chantal and I, of course, grew increasingly more comfortable with each other, ever more familiar and friendly. There were kisses on the cheek and occasional pats on the shoulder or back, but psychically as well as physically, we maintained a platonic distance between us.

More than anything else in the world, I wanted to hold her hand, put my nose into her hair and inhale, kiss her neck. But I was deathly afraid that the slightest move, like a record scratch, would derail what was the most transfixing connection I'd ever had with a human being in my life.

Despite being in generally high spirits, from time to time my mind wandered, and I would tell myself that someone like me, who was so disfigured on the inside, would never be good enough for someone as angelic and naturally buoyant as Chantal. So, aware that I was never far from screwing up and plunging myself into yet another anguish, I was fastidious in taking care to *never* cross any boundary that would even signal any of my true feelings. I quelled those feelings, knowing that after having the best month of my life, one wrong move could send me back to the dark place from which I had emerged, and I understood how, having tasted happiness, that darkness would be exponentially more devastating than before, possibly something I wouldn't be able to survive.

CAHOOTS

I was certain Chantal knew nothing about my true feelings. She was unjaded, a person who always saw the best in people and didn't assume impure motives. I figured she considered me a friend, perhaps one for whom she felt a growing fondness, or, as I suspected, at least someone in transition whom she could help.

This assessment was confirmed for me after we had overkilled the research phase but, thanks to my meandering indecision, still hadn't approved any ideas to execute. I could tell she was becoming frustrated by my holding up the process, and although she gave no such indication, I feared she might professionally dump me.

In what I suppose was her last-ditch effort, she invited me to a brainstorming lunch to settle on ideas by extracting my inner inspiration. We met at her favorite coffee shop, a Japanese spot covered from floor to ceiling in imported wood. As Chantal had been born in Tokyo, she claimed this place helped her think. We sat down at a huge communal table—the only two people—and even before the waitress came by, Chantal revealed her hunch that I was holding creative juices within me that were just waiting to burst free. She stared at me squarely out of her humongous, perpetually wide-open brown eyes and asked me to name my heroes. These, she suggested, could be characters Rosenberg and I could pay homage to by dressing up as or in some way emulating.

Since I was still struggling to understand who I was, let alone who my heroes were, the simple question left me feeling flustered, and I remained mute, just staring at the treated wooden walls. Then, in a pathetic start, I heard myself stutter, take a breath, and blurt out, "Jane Goodall, David Bowie, Mr. Rogers, Gandhi, and Winnie the Pooh"—names that were both revealing and surprising, especially to me.

"I love those answers," Chantal replied. "How do you think you and Rosenberg might go about portraying any of them?"

Having asked the question, she naturally grew silent and waited for me to answer.

I felt even more stumped, and my stomach suddenly tightened; sweat formed on my neck and lower back, and I froze again. My entire world closed in on me as I realized that despite my religious zeal to accomplish our vision, apart from failing to write a book, I hadn't done anything creative since art class in third grade—and I had pretty much forgotten what that was.

I now felt both fraudulent and humiliated. My tightened stomach began to twitch, sweat began to flow in rivulets down my back, and my mind raced, searching for answers. I knew if I didn't say something soon, she would finally see me as the defective person I was and simply throw me away. The silence was painfully awkward for us both as I turned my usual feelings of self-loathing inward.

But this time turned out to be different.

I suddenly and inexplicably did the exact opposite of what I was accustomed to. In a complete about-face, *I let my emotions out and told her the truth.* And the truth was that as a failed writer, I was never and could never be a creative person, so if we were to continue together on this project, she would have to carry all the creative weight.

The frown on her face told me I had screwed up. Clearly, I had touched a nerve, the *wrong* nerve. I was just about to beat her to the punch and call quits on our joint project when she smiled slightly, opened her lovely mouth, and delivered an endearing and in no way patronizing monologue that has never stopped affecting my life to this day.

"First of all, everyone is born creative, so what you just said isn't possible. Your problem is society categorizes us all into little boxes—left-brained or right-brained—when in fact everyone is cranially ambidextrous. Every decision we make, no matter how imaginative or how mundane—what we choose to say or not say, how we cook, what we read, even how we brush our teeth—requires creativity. Life is a blank canvas, and you need to hack your programming that conditions you to stay in a lane, because staying in a lane goes against your natural propensity to think freely, imaginatively, artistically. You need to find ways to detach from social pressures to get out of the lane you're stuck in and move into a whole different lane."

As if it had been rehearsed ahead of time, at this exact second, Rosenberg rolled around on his back as if he were break dancing and let out a deeply pitched, pleasure-affirming howl.

We both laughed.

"See what I mean?" Chantal asked. "Our creativity emerges when we embrace our own universe. Another reason we need to be more like our dogs: they live free and never judge others or themselves—ideal for creative thinking."

"That makes sense in theory," I allowed. "But isn't it much harder in practice since we are governed by our old habits and imprinted pathological insecurities?" This was a phrase I had picked up in therapy. "Did you ever have any of those?" I wondered aloud.

She looked at me rather mischievously, smiled, and conceded that she did. "We all do, which is why it's important to develop our own personal *tricks.*"

Her first trick, she said, was simple. Developed over years, perhaps accelerated by having endured her father's death at such a young age, this trick was teaching herself that since life can be unpredictable and tough, never dwell on things you have no ability to control.

I watched her eyes scanning mine before she added, "I hope this doesn't sound pretentious, but my second trick is always make an effort to be wearable art."

I looked at her outfit—blue-and-purple suede boots, black diamond-patterned tights, a midlength rainbow Missoni dress, and a flatteringly fitted black leather motorcycle jacket.

"Wearing bright colors," she went on to say, "juxtaposing different pieces, and creating a visual spectacle brightens my mood, makes me feel free. It even boosts others' moods. It's entertaining, a creative catalyst. Anything and everything can be a canvas. How you paint that canvas can be a reminder and an enabler—for both you and others—to see the poetry in everyday life.

"Why don't you take some fashion risks?" she suggested. "Wear something that inspires you." She reminded me about the computer avatars chosen by the characters in *The Matrix*—a screenwriter's take on seeing yourself as you have always dreamed—saying different clothing might help me see myself in my more natural, creative light and help give us the attention we needed for our work.

I suddenly realized that, as far back as I could remember, I had dressed in muted earth tones—a good, simple way to blend in and not call attention to myself. I also considered how I had so often judged people who wore clothes that stood out, thinking they were just looking for attention, and thought those who were into fashion were just a bunch of superficial materialists. Now, entering Chantal's world, I began to reframe one pessimistic judgment after another. I also began to kick myself, figuratively, for being so closed-minded and ignorant.

Then I just kept going down the wormhole, cataloging other thoughts, opinions, and judgments I had harbored about people. It wasn't just that these were mean, though they were, and I regretted the meanness; it was also that harboring such judgments prevented me from enjoying life, literally kept me from interacting with others and thereby surrounding myself with the extraordinary qualities and talents of different people.

In acknowledging this, I realized I was still changing as a person, still growing up. I made a pledge to myself to break the restrictive mold I had been in and, from this point on, to stop judging people—starting, perhaps most importantly, with myself.

I felt a new clarity, as if there in the Japanese coffee shop with its wooden walls I had just leveled up in my transformation.

I told Chantal that while it might take time, I would take her advice and become more fashionably adventurous. In the meantime, though, I begged her to keep her title of wardrobe consultant and put me in any crazy colors she could think of.

We had reached a mutual understanding, and a mutually understood, if not completely acknowledged, creative artery had been unblocked.

We wrapped up our lunch meeting by locking in a few concepts, making plans to purchase props and costumes, and ironing out a detailed plan to officially start our work.

Chapter 13

The Dog Dad Rises

IT'S BOTH FRUSTRATING AND ODDLY satisfying when clichés, preconceived opinions, or widely held beliefs hold true. Yet this happens all too often, occurring almost as consistently as death, taxes, and the reality that things can always get worse. And since baked into the human condition is the belief that our thoughts, perspectives, convictions, and experiences are each as one-of-a-kind as a snowflake, no matter how many times we learn it, no matter how many times we look back and realize it was mercilessly obvious all along, we still forget it every damn time: what *is* true *holds* true.

My personal favorite among these certitudes—because I follow it least—is the principle known as Occam's razor: "The simplest explanation is usually the best one." Or, like we heard in school, KISS: keep it simple, stupid. Its truth is so basic, so logical, so helpful, so clearly applicable to almost any situation that it does make one wonder why we perpetually disregard it. Perhaps it's because of our uniquely romantic ability to dream, make mistakes, go off the reservation—the things that catalyze many of the accidents that light our lives with happiness and drive human ingenuity and forward progress. Perhaps this is just what makes us human, enabling us to be simultaneously the masters of our planet and the cannibals bringing about its destruction.

It was this failure to follow the Occam's razor principle that kept Chantal and me overcomplicating our ideas and looking for convoluted solutions to reach our creative goals as we worked to bring our first round of photos to life. Mistakenly, we aimed for the highest of highfalutin goals, which, given that our work was in its infancy, were simply not possible to achieve.

After much frustration, and much fanfare, we dropped the complicated concepts involving elaborate costumes, props, sets, and scenarios and reduced my identity to its authentic essence: Topher Brophy, the proud Dog Dad who loved his son more than anything and wanted to be the best father he could be.

I actually found the perfect definition on Urban Dictionary: "A dog dad is the proud owner of a dog and loves his dog like he would love his own kids—if he had any. Dog dads will eagerly tell anyone who will listen about the random mundanities of his dog's life, even if no one asked. Dog dads get minted at any age, whether it's adopting a new puppy or rescuing a senior dog to live a good life in comfort."

I had only one key correction: the use of the word "owner." Implying that dogs are property and subservient to us made me shudder. I would change "proud owner of a dog" to "proud parent of a dog."

This definition pretty much crystallized our first round of ideas, so we finally went to work in my makeshift living room/photography studio. No complicated costumes, no intricate props, no set design. Instead, Rosenberg and I, in our matching outfits, sourced and constructed by Chantal, just let our love shine. In one weekend we shot five setups portraying what a normal father and son would do: eat breakfast together, read bedtime stories, play sports, cook, and partake in bath time. We respected both Occam's razor and KISS by keeping the captions straightforward and unadorned. There was no rehashing of my life story, the ups and downs of my sorrows, or my road to redemption. Step one was in progress: we were going to get people to look.

Once the photos were shot, we posted them all immediately on the newly created @topherbrophy Instagram account, using what we deemed to be the appropriate hashtags—#DogDad, #ProudDad, #MySon, #MyBoy, and #DogsAreFamily.

Mere minutes after we uploaded the photos, hundreds of people found our account, presumably by searching for the hashtags, and they began commenting, tagging their fellow dog-loving friends, and asking questions about us and our work. We responded as quickly as we could to this almost-instant reaction, which helped us lock in concepts for the next round of photos.

The next weekend we wanted to focus on adding visual variety, so we moved outside to shoot a father-and-son swimming lesson, a leisurely drive, a track workout, and a dressage competition—all pretty high-toned and all with Rosenberg and me adorned in a Chantal original, uniquely crafted for each particular event.

This time we did not post all the photos at once as we had before. Instead, we spaced them out, one per day at just about eight thirty each morning. Since that's when people typically start their day, we thought the early posting would maximize traction. In two weeks' time—it seemed like overnight to us—we had more than two thousand followers. Many of them sent emails and direct messages asking questions, affirming that they, too, considered their dogs and cats children, proclaiming they loved our work, and begging us to continue posting new photos.

We also began receiving memes followers had made, including photoshopped versions of our work that put Rosenberg's head on my body and vice versa. We heard from some followers that we were on the front page of Reddit, and the day after that, we received a professionally produced video from Condé Nast of all our photos set to music, with captions identifying our Instagram handle and video views in the millions. We had gone viral.

That same week saw the first occasion Rosenberg and I were recognized by a total stranger, something I will never forget. After a long walk over the Williamsburg Bridge, which connects Brooklyn to the Lower East Side of Manhattan, we had stopped in a bodega where I intended to refill Rosenberg's water and buy myself a kombucha. There was a long line at the deli counter, mainly because a hard-hatted construction worker—with a six-foot, five-inch frame that shouted PHYSICAL POWER AND MANLINESS—was ordering what sounded like fifteen sandwiches; clearly, it was his turn to bring back lunch to the construction site. In the middle of placing his order, he happened to look back at the line stretched behind him and caught my eye. He stopped ordering and headed our way, at which point this looming tower of toughness asked if he could please take a photo of us.

I was taken aback and must have looked it, so he justified his request by telling me it was for his wife, who, he said, "loved" us. He went on to say the two of them treated *their* dog like a son, too, and they both loved him more than anything in the world. Hearing this, I picked up Rosenberg in our most natural and signature pose—where I hold him as if he is sitting like a human, upright and leaning on me with his head and eyes level to mine—smiled wide, thanked the guy profusely, and asked him to send his wife our love for being a fan.

What I felt after that encounter is, to this day, hard to describe. Surreal is probably the best adjective, but elated, embarrassed, and proud—all fused together—*almost* does justice to my feelings. What most surprised me was that this man, who in every outward way epitomized the macho modern male archetype known for catcalling women, publicly stopped what he was doing to ask for a photo and talk about how much he loved his dog. I was still processing what this meant when it became clear to me that we were on our way, much faster than we had anticipated, to hitting a nerve. It meant, I believed, we were achieving what we had set out to do—but we still had a long way to go.

As the laws of momentum dictate, luck begets luck, a crowd attracts a crowd, and affirmation increases one's conviction. A strange feeling began to germinate in me—strange because it felt simultaneously foreign and completely natural. Ideas, opinions, and points of view I had never had or understood before began to make sense to me; in fact, they almost shone with clarity. It wasn't until later, looking back, that I realized what I was feeling—for the first time in my life—was confidence, a level of self-assurance I had never experienced.

This ignited a burst of creative ideas for our work and with that, a therapy of sorts that filled in—with a new, sharp clarity—who I had been in the past, who I wanted to be in the future, how I wanted to be seen, and how I might actually in some way affect the world I lived in, a world that was suddenly opening up before me. My encounter with the construction worker showed me, among so much else, that there were countless people in the world whose daily work was essential to our everyday lives. I now saw that as heroic; at the same time, I saw it as unconscionable that these workers did not receive the recognition, appreciation, and respect they deserved. It occurred to me that we could play a part in turning that around, so our next series portrayed Rosenberg and me as teachers, construction workers, firefighters, veterans, nurses, UPS drivers, and police officers. Our captions detailed the ways we almost literally could not live without these people, thanked them for doing what they did, and asked everyone else to join us in recognizing them as the real celebrities of our society. We referred to this series as our Humble Homage, and to this day, it remains an integral part of our work.

As we continued to post various professions and corresponding hashtags, an entirely new crowd of followers emerged. It wasn't just people who loved dogs anymore; it was also people who worked in these occupations, as well as their friends and family members, commenting and tagging one another in the posts, spreading the message of appreciation and recognition, and creating a feedback loop of affection and positive energy.

We were helping people feel good about their professions and appreciated for their work. If we could help do that, I thought, wouldn't those people feel happier and therefore be nicer to others? And might that, in turn, contribute in even some small way to making the world a better place?

At the same time we were posting this series—the summer of 2016—American politics took over our lives. The candidate who had won the Republican nomination unleashed a series of insults, misinformation, fear tactics, and generally unethical behavior that sent the media and then the general public into a state of near hysteria. Media coverage of this heightened state of national emotion, as it often does, encouraged a wave of fear, pessimism, and panic.

After weeks of this media recycling, the public was hungry for positivity and anything that could counterbalance the dark cloud that seemed to be looming over the whole nation. In search of just about any lighthearted distraction they could get, people found themselves turning to images of a man who looked and dressed like his dog.

Rosenberg and I stepped up to the plate and fit the bill—perfectly. We were compelling enough and simultaneously projected so profoundly important a message that we could not fail to resonate with a public exhausted by anger and negativity. And so we received inquiries from various publications—not just in the United States but also from almost every hemisphere—asking to use our photos on their sites *and* to interview or profile us.

As someone who had identified himself as a functional recluse for most of his life, the sudden influx of attention was bewildering, intimidating, flattering, and tantalizing all at once. With so many media inquiries coming in, I didn't have time to answer all my DMs, emails, and comments from our followers—now numbering more than ten thousand—while also ideating and shooting more photos with Chantal and, most importantly, cooking and hand-feeding Rosenberg his meals and taking him out for the minimum three hours of anaerobic exercise he needed and deserved. I felt I was continually walking off the edge of a cliff, and while with every step, the ground miraculously followed me underfoot, I was sure I was only one small misstep from falling into the infinite expanse below.

At the same time, every cog in my brain and all my synapses were firing perfectly. I loved every second of the gratification that came from the animal parents from all walks of life who were now constantly reaching out to us. Many simply thanked us and told stories about how animal companions improved their lives. But there were others—some in cancer treatment, some suffering from a terminal illness, some who had just lost a human or animal relative—who told us we had given them their first smile in weeks. To me these connections were a hundred times more impactful than therapy. They were like a car defroster, clearing the fog from a windshield. It didn't matter that I didn't know any of these people; each exchange felt like I was sharing a vein to their suffering, a suffering that was universal and analogous to mine. This was proof that we all wanted to make the world a better place.

But while I would lie in bed contemplating that I might actually be becoming the person I had always wanted to be, I also contemplated the converse: that I was, as Nietzsche had described, blind to reality and just another sheep in the herd. I was a guy who happened to resemble his astounding dog and had used that to glom on to a vapid fad, a guy who had caught the wave of a particular moment at just the right time when people needed an escape. Perhaps I was actually on the precipice of mania and only felt this flow of satisfaction and power because I kept myself so busy that there was simply no room for the demons who actually ruled my psyche to make it to the head of the line. Perhaps my days of online fame were numbered.

Yet I couldn't shake the thought that things that had never made sense before were beginning to seem intelligible, *meaningful*. Things like how people relate to one another, how the mind works, how the world works. I saw patterns where I had never seen patterns before—templates that showed how to be consciously alive or at least how other people were consciously alive. *This means something!* I thought. *So this is how it's done! I get it now!*

I had no idea what was coming next or how whatever it turned out to be would play out. I was well aware, however, that the current media frenzy was either the biggest opportunity for us to take this to an entirely new and different level or that it was about to crash and burn us into oblivion, sending all my dreams into the hellish purgatory that was perpetually awaiting me.

Chapter 14

"Fake News"

WE OF THE *HOMO SAPIENS* species tend to assume our big brains govern our behavior, but the truth is our instincts still lead us to act like pack animals. We see this most clearly when we observe large groups, but it is actually noticeable in almost every part of our lives. Humans conform to the norms, opinions, behaviors, and practices that represent the prevailing culture of the place and time in which we live, and we do so while being blissfully unaware of the transience of that culture. Such conformity is a likely by-product of our evolution; it helps us maintain order, sustain productivity, and make progress in innumerable ways. At the same time, however, such conformity has its pitfalls: like it or not, we are prone to follow others without questioning our behavior.

Since the advent of the printing press, reading the written word in various forms of mass communication—that is, the media—has had a profound influence on the opinions, belief systems, and accepted perspectives that influence human behavior. It is clear that our most recent technological revolution has transformed the mediascape to the point where clicks, shares, and profits are prioritized over facts and objectivity. Yes, this has happened before—just check out the yellow journalism of the nineteenth century, which kicked off the whole sordid phenomenon of sensationalism. But today's yellow journalism reaches an exponentially larger audience and moves so fast that it makes us far more susceptible to being manipulated into groupthink.

Before I tell how I became a subject of media scrutiny, I want to be clear right from the outset that I am in no way maligning the media, journalism, or journalists. There is a reason the press is the only profession protected in the United States Constitution—it's an essential pillar of our freedom and democracy. So I'm with Thomas Jefferson when he said he'd rather have a free press without a government than a government without a free press.

I'd also like to acknowledge that the motive of these writers was to report on pop culture as a distraction and amusement. As a subject, a man who dresses like his dog is not likely to score a Pulitzer, and the reporters interested in covering such a subject were by no means gunning for one, even though my life's work felt Pulitzer-worthy to me.

Finally, since the goal of our—yes, Chantal and I were now a team, in the business sense at least—project was to promote our cause to as many people as possible, we were and will forever be grateful to have been (and to still be) a subject of interest to any publication that will have us. From the start, press coverage helped us move forward toward our ultimate aim. Unfortunately, our na-ivete and gratitude for such coverage led to a somewhat unhealthy blind trust in the press.

We considered the media interest in what we were doing to be our big break. For us the stakes could not have been higher, and we believed if we played it just right, if we did it successfully, it could open up more opportunities for us to spread our message even more widely than we could have dreamed.

And as such, our first media inquiry seemed to ignite count-less others of the same type from around the world. This first wave came mostly from publications we hadn't heard of before with clev-er names that sounded internet-ish, but because we were so flat-tered to be of interest to them at all, to us they felt like the *New York Times*. The inquiries typically came from someone with a ti-tle—a senior journalist or photo editor—who was so intrigued by our project that they "felt compelled to reach out via email." The titled email writer typically opened with a compliment, then list-ed the many publications they worked for, and ended by seeking permission to use our photos. The *yes!* we routinely provided was invariably met with an instant reply that included a photo release contract, which, we were told, had to be sent back ASAP in order to meet the publication's deadline.

We felt rushed, but we carefully read the small print, where we found a clause giving the publication the legal right to repurpose or resell the photos it would use. We asked all our eager emailers precisely what this meant, and all answered, as if in unison, that the clause was "mere boilerplate that didn't apply to us." *Ignore it*, they assured us.

Naive we may have been, but we were also suspicious and pushed back, declaring we would agree to sign *only* if the publication promised every photo of ours they used would be accompanied by a written statement that would explain the mission of our work. All agreed! So we signed on the dotted line, as the saying goes, and figured we were on our way.

Days later, multiple articles came out online at the same time—but not in the reputable publications the writers claimed to have worked for. Instead, the articles and our photos were all over a range of tabloids in sections like "News of the Bizarre!" with headlines that screamed "1% Dog Has Bigger Wardrobe Than Man!" simultaneously placing Rosenberg among the wealthiest in our society and making me look like a complete idiot.

In short, we were presented as a freakish novelty, and there was no mention whatsoever of our mission or message. Crushed by having been misled, we went back to the people who had reached out to us in the first place. Turns out that these "senior journalists" and "photo editors" actually worked at various photo agencies for which they basically offered stories they found to a range of sources. It was, they told us, just a matter of happenstance that a bunch of—somewhat, shall we say, less-than-serious—sites happened to pick up the story about us.

Our followers on social media, still a rapidly growing group, found many of these articles and sent them to us. They also let us know our photos were being used in countless advertisements—our likeness popping up all over the internet—without permission having been asked for or granted. It turned out we were also appearing in random clickbait ads for telecom companies and for selling dog products in countries overseas. We even showed up on billboards in Eastern Europe, saying who knows what in languages I couldn't read or understand.

And that was only the beginning. Catalyzed by this lowbrow onslaught of exposure, articles about us began to surface in all sorts of places. The first was written by an activist from the animal rights organization PETA. The article accused us of animal cruelty for dressing Rosenberg in human clothes, and it suggested he should be rescued from us and placed where he could receive more responsible care. Then came an article on an evangelical news site. It detailed the unraveling of the nuclear family and of traditional values and claimed people like us, who consider our pets children, were in large part responsible for this degeneration. It found us guilty of encouraging others to engage in unwholesome lifestyles and of deliberately advocating against having human kids. We had now become a threat to upright families everywhere.

This crushing succession of missteps and the disasters that followed led us to stop—abruptly—any and all responses to any and all written publications. It had been made abundantly clear to us that we weren't able to control the narratives they let loose. Instead, we decided to accept an in-person TV interview with a lovely woman who reached out to us from Fox News. Because we would obviously do most of the talking, we felt pretty certain there was no way our words could get twisted.

We were on high alert anyway, but when our interviewer walked into the apartment, Chantal, whose facial expressions and body language I was able to read by now, and I felt instantly at ease. She was tall and wore a casual but stylish knee-length brown-and-red dress dotted with small white circles. And since, at Chantal's direction, Rosenberg and I were dressed in matching red tank tops and white yoga pants, our colors perfectly matching hers, we felt an instant sense of closeness. She also offered a big smile and hugged us in a big-sister sort of way before exchanging small talk—mostly about the neighborhood, which, as a Queens native, she had never been to before, and about her daughter, who was, for this single mother, the love of her life.

So our guard was definitely down as the interview began. Predictably, our interviewer started off with questions about how we got started and why I refer to Rosenberg as my son and not as my pet. Then she asked how we get ideas and inspiration for our work. These were certainly rational questions aimed at seeking objective information, and I was happy to provide the answers, working in some aspects of my backstory along with articulating our mission and end goal: to bring people together and make the world a better place.

But after about fifteen minutes, our interviewer's tone suddenly changed, and so did the nature of her questions. I detected a note of sarcasm in her voice when she asked how much money we spend on Rosenberg's wardrobe and whether I thought animals were more important than people. I tried to deflect this line of questioning, but she persisted, asking what I did to make a living that allowed me to pay for this lovely apartment, the photography equipment, and all the expensive props required to do our work. I explained that I had once worked in sales, and when the company I worked for was purchased by a Silicon Valley competitor at the height of the dot-com boom, I put the money I received from the buyout into real estate. Ever since, I told her, I had learned how to grow that original investment exponentially. Not satisfied with this answer, she talked over me, suggesting I was a trust-fund kid, which of course was not the case.

So I tried to change the subject. I talked about my past emotional struggles and my history of narcissism to try to bring the story back to the goal of the Instagram account.

"Define narcissism," she demanded, "and elaborate on it—in particular on your selfishness."

I began to answer, but she soon seemed bored and abruptly changed course once again, asking about the yoga pants Rosenberg and I were wearing. She wanted to know if we practiced yoga, and if so, would I do a few poses, chants, or meditations. So I did, holding Rosenberg in our signature pose as she zoomed in on his face.

"Let's wrap this up with just a few more questions," she said and proceeded to ask about the nature of our relationship with social media and @thedogstyler before, seemingly out of left field, asking if I was still a narcissist since, as she put it, all I do is post photos of myself every day.

The question disarmed me, and I could only counter that we used our images as a Trojan horse to gain attention for our cause—an answer that seemed to satisfy her. She then walked around the apartment shooting B-roll, the footage that gets intercut with the main subject of the filming to add color and background. With that done, she transformed back into the warm woman we had met when she walked in, thanked us for our time, and left somewhat abruptly.

Chantal and I felt strange about the interview, but we had no choice but to sit and wait, with bated breath and nerves on edge, for the interview to air.

The following week, as Chantal and I watched it together, our mouths hit the floor. The entire segment was an all-out attack on Rosenberg and me. We were toast, completely and utterly. Right from the get-go, at the very moment our interviewer looked into the live camera, introduced us, and began telling our story, she simply declared it was strange—read weird and freakish—for a man to dress like his dog. Our project, she proclaimed to her vast audience of viewers, was fueled by narcissism, and she ridiculed my claim that narcissism was what I was trying to run away from.

After that excruciating intro, the segment segued into a group of reporters sitting around discussing us as our footage played out on the screen, accompanied by huge graphics calling me a hypocrite and, in big red moving letters, the "Loser of the Week." The piece ended with a shot of me doing the yoga poses and chanting the interviewer had baited us to perform, adding a new-age touch to further paint me as just another narcissistic, millennial sideshow freak.

It is hard to put into words what all this felt like. I experienced a new level of disgust, disappointment, embarrassment, and sheer heartache from watching it. As someone who had finally found a way to feel great and to see the hopeful side of being alive, to be treated so duplicitously was heart-wrenching.

What hurt most was how I had been so open and honest in the interview about everything the tabloid internet had just done to us. I was so sure this interviewer from a reliable, real network would be the opposite of all that, would be a genuine journalist. I had always felt—naively, no doubt—that writers and journalists were, in a way, almost like public servants, seeking truth, exercising impartiality, and aiming to help others. Everyday heroes. But if someone like this could act so deceptively and with such malicious intent, what did this say about the state of our society, human nature, and the future of the world?

The hurt I felt brought back memories of how I had felt most of my life. All of it was still just under my skin, muscle memory. And when it came to the surface, I thought maybe I *was* the "Loser of the Week," and maybe the past few months had just been a fantasy or, worse, a fever dream.

I felt myself drifting back into that familiar funk, closed off and souring against people again.

Chantal sensed this and demanded I talk about it. I told her I needed space, but she would not take no for an answer.

"That isn't possible," she said.

And she persisted. She came over to my place and pushed me until I popped open. I had nowhere to hide, and while my feelings for her were as passionate as ever, against what I thought was my better judgment, I spilled everything. I told her all about the past I had tried to keep hidden from her, how, from the very beginning, I had always felt impotent, and how, through the sum of my experiences, I had always looked down on human nature. I told her how I saw the world.

Patiently, she heard me out, then admitted she, too, felt such feelings at times, but, as she gently put it, "That's life. We can't have the ups without the downs. The things you have been through," she went on to say, "the tough times you've survived are the reason I sense so much depth within you, the reason you relate so well to other people—especially those who are suffering.

"All of that," she said with a smile, "is why you're such an amazing person and why I've fallen in love with you."

From her lips to my ears and into my brain, those words stopped time. I felt as if I were in a vacuum, all alone, in another dimension or an alternate universe. All the feelings of despair evaporated, and in some intangible, surreal way, my entire body grew warm. Apart from my parents and my first puppy-love girlfriend at age fifteen, no one had ever said they loved me before. And now the woman of my dreams, my creative partner, the object of my unfathomably huge crush—which I had kept locked in the center of my soul for fear of rejection—had just bestowed the words upon me. If this was possible, then everything was possible.

I now knew there was nothing I couldn't accomplish with her by my side. At that moment, I knew we became a family: Chantal, Rosenberg, and me.

Chapter 15

Re-re-rebirth

YOU CAN'T HAVE THE UPS *without the downs.* It's an overstated platitude, yet it *is* one of the simplest, most profound, most therapeutic statements ever made. Like lining up at the DMV, this seesaw between high and low is a great leveler. Nobody gets a pass. No matter how smart, successful, or stunning you may be, you, too, will experience sky-high highs and subterranean lows.

For some, myself included, such fluctuations occur more frequently and more sharply than for most people. The lows can feel like a free fall into an end-of-the-world wormhole that offers no way out. The best we can do is wait it out, as if it were a catastrophic storm or a virus running its course. But when we're convinced this manic, living hell is eternal, putting an end to everything can seem like the only logical option. It's hard to remember the light at the end of the tunnel is just around the bend but obscured by fog. One more day, one more hour, one more minute, and the light can break through.

The catastrophic failure of our first venture with the press sent me reeling into just such an abyss of wretchedness. All my hopes and dreams—as well as all meaning, magic, and poetry—were snuffed out. Now that I had tasted the sweet fruit of personal fulfillment, the contrast between low and high was too harrowing to bear.

And then the miracle happened. My best friend—the person I worshipped, the person I secretly and longingly loved, the person I never imagined could or would ever love me—suddenly and without coercion, uttered the most magical words in any language: *I am in love with you.*

It was a lightning bolt that switched on the lights in every cell in my body and caused my synapses to fire faster than machine guns. The result was a high better than any drug. The world had become not just more beautiful but more breathtaking than I had ever imagined it could be. Most revolutionary, though, was *when* she said it— right after I had finally come clean about the emotional struggles that had caused the pockmarked scars of my disfigured psyche. I had assumed my confession would push her away. It was utterly counterintuitive that the opposite occurred, that the peeling back of the last layer of my truth had brought us closer, had opened a new intimacy between us.

Finally, she knew who I truly was. Why didn't she flee? Because as a pure person, way more evolved and enlightened than I was, she knew that as humans, we are all broken, and only when we reach a certain level of self-understanding are we able to acknowledge it, to appreciate and understand that this pathology—this endless searching for happiness and creating meaning—is what makes us beautiful.

Rationally, I understand that this is the case, that this is real. But because of my pathology, even after being with Chantal for, as I write this, just shy of a decade, the idea of another person accepting me, loving me, and tolerating my presence is at times still utterly incomprehensible.

Thankfully, the rational part of my brain is robust enough to keep these demons at bay. I'm able to see how I and others who go through life in a perpetually stalemated game of chicken puff up our chests, trying to convince others and ourselves we have everything under control. "Hey! We got this! We are whole! We are good to go!" We repress emotions, keeping our upper lips so stiff they feel like calluses of steel. Blind to the magic our vulnerability can offer, we hide our humanness at all costs, preventing connection and blocking the pathway for letting another person in.

As someone who never imagined I could be loved, I direct this stern statement to any reader who has ever felt, deep down, they aren't good enough, attractive enough, smart enough, or desirable enough to be worthy of another person's love. That is simply not true, and I have the proof—I am the king of emotional catastrophes, and somebody loves me.

This does not mean you are *not* a flawed disaster. It means *we are all flawed disasters.* This is also what makes us all beautiful. You have my word and my promise that if you desire such a thing, someone can and will love you.

I used to think finding love would take away my pain by pacifying my demons and making me complete, a whole human who could experience the full range of emotions. After all, doesn't our culture—through books and movies and, heaven knows, television commercials—assure us that all we need in life is a partner and everything will be absolutely perfect forever? Fall in love, and your troubles are over; you can look ahead to an angst-free lifetime. But guess what? It's a fallacy. The god you're looking for, the magic you seek, the completion of self you thought you would find in another person is an illusion, another of those great big jokes the universe tends to play on emotional disasters like me.

The truth is that the magic we are looking for—the alchemy that can transform us—is found within. We are all born with it. It is baked into our DNA. The only way to turn it on is to go deep, identify it, unlock it, then harness its power. It may take a lifetime to find it, mine it, and unleash its potential into our everyday existence, but once we do, we can live, truly live, feeling complete within ourselves and, if we choose, in a partnership.

How did I find my magic? Simple. Rosenberg's unconditional love was the battery that jump-started my love generator. Once I dedicated myself to him, I was able to break free from narcissism and gain back my sense of self. To become the dog dad he deserved, I had to shatter my emotional armor and unlock my full range of emotions. I came to understand I had an indulgently empathic and perpetually bleeding heart. If harnessed properly, as I believe it now is, it can become my greatest strength instead of my cosmic curse. It led to the discovery of my mission in life, filled my days with meaning, enabled me to let my guard down and, for the first time in my entire life, receive love.

Yes, getting here took me through a labyrinth, and I surely ran the full gamut of human emotions. But now, beyond doubt, I live a life much larger than myself and far more rewarding than I could ever have imagined. Everyone can. It may take some of us a little longer to unlock the magic within us, but it is always there.

If I hadn't, Chantal the Dog Styler, who was already my best friend, might not have told me she loved me. And I might not have done the same in return.

Thanks to Rosenberg forcing me to uncover my magic, I found the love of my life, and he found his mom.

With Rosenberg at our side, Chantal and I fast-forwarded through all the typical relationship milestones. We had our family. Nothing more was needed. The media debacle became a joke we could laugh at, water running off a duck's back. Our project was *so* not ruined, we decided. On the contrary, we would learn from this mistake and create our own narrative as a tribe of three, united by the impenetrable armor of fluffy fur love. We would do what we had always wanted to do: help people, try to change the world, and possibly kick up some dust doing it.

Chapter 16

The Big Payback

As THIS HUMBLE BOOK HAS tried to make clear from the start, my most seminal struggle has been the discrepancy between the person I wanted to be and the reality of who I was and how I related to the world. The idealized version of myself, a composite of heroes my brain gobbled up in biographies, fiction, and movies, was a leader who acted with the integrity of a knight who gave to the needy—à la Robin Hood—offered a voice to the voiceless, and unlike everyone else on earth, was immune to social pressures as he went about always acting selflessly to make the world a better place. I was devoted to high ideals and driven by the desire to live up to the values I embraced, but I was also utterly incapable of *acting*. I could feel the pain of others but just had no idea how to respond to such pain.

After the roller coaster of ups and downs that had characterized my life up to this point in the story, I found myself, for the first time ever, deeply rooted and firmly planted in solid ground. I not only had a mission, a cause to believe in, but I also now had self-esteem. I had a wonderful, noble, and beautiful son and a kind, creative genius who actually loved me. This all felt too good to be true, but it was true, and the truth of it awakened in me the sense that if I were ever to become even an inkling of the person I wanted to be, now was the time. If I were ever going to be able to look up to myself, even for a moment; if I were ever going to aim toward the ideals of the heroes I had read about in religious texts, myths, fiction, and fables; if I were ever going to find meaning and satisfaction in life despite the inevitability of my death, this was it.

There was only one next step that made sense: philanthropy, the only thing that always made the world a better place. Of course, we had no experience in this vast field, but we did have a raucous amount of energy, and with necessity acting as the mother of invention, my gut was telling me exactly how to go about it.

With Chantal's close collaboration and blessing, I began getting in touch with charities dedicated to causes we both believed in. The process was surprisingly simple: I would research the charity online, identify one that touched me, look up its rating at www. charitynavigator.org to determine its legitimacy, then find the organization's press representative or public relations contact, and reach out. In my email I identified who we were, showed samples of our work, provided a profile of our following, and stated the personal reasons why we were passionate about the organization's cause. We ended our "pitch" by saying we would love to treat the organization as a pro bono client and shoot a photo to promote it on our social media feeds to help raise money and awareness for their cause.

Because charities are always looking for exposure and donations, every organization we reached out to responded with a big and enthusiastic yes. Often the people working for these organizations were volunteers themselves, many with a personal connection to the cause, so they were deeply appreciative of our desire to help. Each charity sent us promotional materials: branded clothing, signage, backdrops, stickers—all sorts of items emblazoned with the organization's name and mission.

Chantal then incorporated these items, along with special guests the charities put us in touch with, into our photos, employing her usual outlandish, attention-grabbing art direction and styling. When posting each photo, I introduced the charity, honored all our participants, made my own personal donation, and asked everyone who was able to do the same and/or, if touched by our post, to promote the cause themselves.

The first organization we officially worked with was NDSS, National Down Syndrome Society, which supports people and families affected by this disorder. NDSS connected us with the parents of Nico and Charlie, and everyone came to our home studio for the photo shoot. Chantal dressed Rosenberg, the boys, and me in matching suits with gold suspenders, and we all had huge grins on our faces—Rosenberg included—which really made everything pop. The kids loved Rosenberg and the photo, which we gifted to the organization and which helped raise money for NDSS. This shoot is still among our favorites to date.

With the ice broken and Veterans Day approaching, we contacted the National Amputation Foundation. For this shoot the foundation connected us with Artie, a gregarious, kind man and still a fond friend who had lost an arm in service to his country. For this photo, Chantal brought in Scooby, an adorable mixed-breed pup missing the same limb as Artie, and dressed all the participants in the photo in military fatigues. We saluted in unison to honor all the brave souls, human and canine, who served our great country, thanking them profusely for their sacrifice and asked our followers to join us by donating to this most worthy endeavor.

Our third shoot, was for the National Organization for Albinism and Hypopigmentation, which connected us with the parents of brothers Chris and Andrew, who have albinism. We paired them with Salvatore the Chihuahua, who, while not albino, had very similar coloring to the boys. Chantal dressed us all in gingham shirts and red pants, with blue sweaters around our necks. We all hugged, with Rosenberg in the middle, for a photo that garnered a lot of attention and donations for the cause.

We kept going with this work, both worthwhile and worthy in our eyes, producing photo shoots and helping raise money for Alzheimer's research, transgender rights, brain cancer (the disease that had taken Chantal's father), natural catastrophe relief, and various children's charities.

By a thousand landslides, doing this work, which directly came to the aid of others and, I believe, helped make the world a better place, did more for my sense of self than anything I had ever done before. It is hard to put succinctly into words the sense of self-respect it brought me. Maybe the best way to describe it is what one of the hundred self-help books I had read called flow—when you are doing the right thing, in the right place, at the right time, and are so engaged in the activity that nothing could possibly tear you away or distract you from it. I imagine this is how our pups feel every second of the day—twenty-four hours of flow. What a wonderful place to be.

Further adding to our high from doing this work was the reaction it inspired among our following, which continued to grow exponentially. The outpouring of love, donations, and support kept gushing, and that touched us deeply. We had the sense that this work was helping to turn on some lights for people who, despite being fatigued or down about struggles in their life, felt a need to help improve the world. We started to feel that our platform proved how goodness could be infectious.

Emboldened by the satisfaction I took from this, I began, in addition to the organizational philanthropic work, to insert more of myself, my struggles in the past, and the lessons I had learned into our posts. Chantal, who at this point knew every last detail of what I had gone through, was quite possibly even more impassioned about this new direction for our content than I was. She came up with wildly creative, outrageous outfits and color-coordinated backdrops, set design, and props to match each idea and sentiment in attention-grabbing ways. These photo shoots and long corresponding captions covered mental illness, narcissism, feeling like an outcast, loneliness, being called weird, why it's okay for men to cry, having learning disabilities, suffering confidence issues, and the power of introverts. For each topic my goal was to ensure that people who had once felt these feelings or were going through them now would know they were neither the first nor the only individuals to suffer as they have suffered, and that they were not alone.

The flood of comments and messages from this line of posts was unprecedented. I received literally thousands of thank-you messages, confessions of individual struggles, and statements from so many people who could relate. What was perhaps even more remarkable, though, was that countless individuals responded to one another about their experiences. It felt almost like an online therapy session and support group, in which people were eager to show kindness, empathy, and understanding—a mass desire to help one another. To me this was perhaps the ultimate certainty that in our own way, we were making a difference for people, that we were doing something that could truly make the world a better place.

And just at that moment, when we felt we had hit our stride, an opportunity presented itself. It was nothing we could have predicted, and it sent us on a soul search, questioning the very foundation of our mission.

Chapter 17

Crossroads

We make hundreds of decisions all day long. Certainly, many of these decisions are banal, requiring barely a thought, while others are complex with potentially weighty consequences; these require careful analysis, research, contemplation, the meticulous weighing of pros and cons, and often seeking advice from people we trust. Yet however simple or complex the thought process behind it, the decision we deem the right one is almost always the one that produces an instinctive, visceral reaction we feel in our gut. It is when we are unable to "read" this reaction—to discern what it is telling us—that the scenario becomes most precarious. Equally unsettling is to receive a clear gut reaction but find our rationality pulling us toward an opposite outcome.

This is what invariably happens to me when I am in pursuit of a larger goal. A fork in the road presents itself; the fork that feels right is the one that would serve the larger purpose, *but* at the same time, following it would require negating a personal conviction or breaking a moral code. What to do?

Valuing integrity above all, I have typically erred on the side of extreme caution. My aim has been to not betray myself in such a way as to eradicate the only source of self-esteem I have and thereby crush my already tenuous relationship with the universe. Back in high school, when my main goal was to make friends, I was careful to avoid interacting with anyone who seemed to me a slave to such superficial matters as clothes, looks, or being "cool." The same applied to people I came across later in life, including those of the opposite sex who may have even been interested in getting to know me. I quickly disqualified any one of them who did not rise to my standards of what constituted the moral high ground—anyone who cheated on a boyfriend or girlfriend or even anyone who got into an exclusive night club and left their group of friends behind. They were to me what *Game of Thrones* termed "oathbreakers." In a world of hypocrites, whose deceits have long pained me, I held onto this self-righteous sanctuary for dear life for way too long.

And of course I did all this judging of others from the sidelines, taking solace in never being a sellout while watching life pass me by. This honorable internal code, as I saw it, was my armor, but instead of protecting me, it actually shielded me from new experiences, preventing me from the chance for human connection, friendship, and romance. It insulated me from what was really just fear of the unknown. In the end, holding onto my self-imposed "purity" was the ultimate act of self-betrayal, stopping me from entering into life itself.

There is a Taoist saying that "the supreme good is like water." It means being able to adapt and evolve to any situation is the surest way to lead a fruitful and fulfilling life. Experience has taught me, finally, that those who wallow in dogmatic codes and fixed principles, those who routinely judge others for selling out, do so out of their own suffering over their debilitating insecurities.

Yet that is precisely how I lived for thirty-plus years until the moment in this story where I faced that classic fork in the road. Even though my gut knew which direction to choose, pathologies are hard to break, and my rational brain put up a monumental fight. What we would not know until later was that the outcome of this decision would dramatically change the trajectory of our project and the course of our lives.

I have noted before in this story—maybe ad nauseam—that for Chantal and me, the point of our work from the very start was to preach the benefits and joys of animal companionship and, through that mission, do whatever we could to make the world a better place. In a society and culture we both saw as overflowing with consumerism, narcissism, divisiveness, and greed, our creative output and the relationship it had created with our "digital family" was the one thing we could keep pure—honorable, true, and downright righteous. That relationship was our safe place. It was why, unlike other social media accounts, we had decided ours would not hawk products, sell T-shirts and calendars, or hook up with big corporations.

We had absolutely nothing against people who did this to make a living, but since our focus was on spreading positivity and raising money for charity, it just wasn't for us.

Then suddenly, out of the blue, a potential client offered us a high-profile opportunity.

Simply put, we were approached by Sprint, who wanted to feature our project in a multimedia advertising campaign. In fact, the campaign had been conceived and written with us in mind. It would serve as a Topher Brophy social media promotional campaign. Yes, it would sell a product, but it would do so by focusing on our message and furthering our mission.

We were taken aback. We were also honored, flattered, and utterly intimidated. After all, working with a large company and selling products went against the very ethos we had worked so hard to establish. So after discussing the matter between us in depth, we were inclined to say no.

But the more we thought about it, the more we saw that if this campaign were to be successful, it had the potential to increase our following considerably, thereby bringing us, with a speed and effectiveness beyond what we could achieve on our own, way closer to achieving our larger goal.

On the other hand, of course, if the campaign flopped and we were taken advantage of, as we had been before, we could almost instantly ruin the purest and most worthwhile thing we had ever done in our lives.

What made the decision-making process even tougher—almost unbearably so—was that the production schedule for the campaign had a rigorously tight timeline, so we had only a few days to provide a formal answer. Bottom line: the clock was ticking toward a no-second-chance deadline for a make-or-break decision.

We searched our souls together and alone hundreds of times, created Venn diagrams, and called our parents and almost everyone we knew, going back and forth from yes to no and back again more times than either of us could count.

I finally decided to say no.

Fortunately, Chantal, possessed of wisdom, foresight, a level head, and better judgment, wouldn't take no for an answer and convinced me to say yes.

We signed the contract, then went right into preproduction. We were off! And I found myself starring in a multifaceted content campaign centered around a "dog dad" commercial.

Having never acted, having never done anything but stand still and have my photo taken by Chantal, I was extraordinarily nervous. The stakes were high, and hundreds of people were involved and counting on me. I was terrified I might let everyone down.

Fortunately, on all levels, the people involved in the production were the utmost professionals. Believe me when I say they are capable of drawing water from a stone. TV production moves fast, yet these folks were extremely patient with me, did and said all the right things, gave me all the right coaching, and succeeded in drawing enough water from this particular stone to pull a good performance out of me.

I was terrified for Rosenberg, though. While he loved dressing up, he tended to get anxious around large groups of people, and large groups of people are unavoidable on a commercial set. Again, these production pros knew exactly what to do. To ease Rosenberg's nerves, they invited his girlfriend, Pippa the Pugalier, to join us on set for the day. Luckily, she let him hump her during every break.

It was a busy day, filled with a range of setups, repeated takes, outfit and location changes—all part of getting everything just right until we finally wrapped up for the day. Some additional voice-over recordings were required, and then it was finished and ready to roll out.

The result was beyond our wildest expectations. The commercial featured Rosenberg and me in elaborate, well-crafted, matching outfits and highlighted our resemblance and the sacredness of our relationship and tied it all together by showing us uploading photos from the newly released phone.

It kept our favorite line—in which I call Rosenberg "my son"—and it was infused with and delivered a heartwarming emotional feeling that celebrated our bond. It was the perfect vehicle for increasing our social media following, and it would succeed in doing just that.

As soon as it was released—in a matter of days—we were seemingly everywhere. Television stations across the country ran our commercial over and over and over again. Almost instantly, our Instagram following increased by a hundred thousand, and countless images of us appeared on new and emerging social platforms, many of which we had not even heard of but which nevertheless begged us to create accounts.

The impact this level of publicity generated was staggering— utterly amazing! Rosenberg and I, on our normal walks around Brooklyn, could go barely a block before a car honked at us or people stopped us in the street and asked to take our picture or even sign an autograph. We weren't accustomed to watching TV or consuming much media at all, but our followers and friends who did told us how they saw our faces all over the internet, on planes, and at sporting events.

It is pretty remarkable to find yourself suddenly ubiquitous. In a sense, we couldn't get away from ourselves. Countless companies— many of them dog-related, but by no means all—contacted us with offers to send us free products, no strings attached. Casting agents for reality television shows, game shows, and morning shows, as well as newspapers and magazines from all over the world contacted us, begging us to be featured or to fill a special guest slot or part. We were flattered, but we turned down all such offers.

While the success of the campaign was thrilling and the resulting attention exciting, what was way more gratifying was, once again, the onslaught of emails from hundreds of people who loved the commercial because they loved their dogs. Like our first go-round with the press, many messages thanked us for validating their referring to their dogs as daughters and sons. Others were grateful we spread positivity, promoted charities, and made them feel better in a world of suffering where, all too often, they felt sad and alone. I replied to all these emails and still to this day diligently exchange messages with their senders, which continues to affect me more profoundly than anything I've ever experienced. That our work and my words provide these folks with some positivity, hope, or just comfort feels to me like an ongoing catharsis and has helped heal the touch points of pain I still carry around and suspect will always be a defining part of me. As different as their stories of suffering may be from my own, they remind me I am not alone. And since being alone is perhaps the scariest thing we have hanging over us in life, the reminder I am not is a gift from these people, and I am profoundly grateful.

Equally significant was how much our attitude toward the media had changed. Where once we had felt taken advantage of by a some-times-cynical press, now, with our mission more actualized and its momentum newly catalyzed, the tables were turned. We had walked the walk now. We had actively helped people's lives and had brought people together. It put us in an extraordinarily happy and playful place. Together with the lessons learned the last time around, this made us realize we had already accomplished way more than we could have dreamed. The bottom line? We had nothing to lose. We had cut the strings of societal pressures, and free-floating over our own steam, we were able to have the most fun we had ever had.

After a lifetime of heaviness, I was consumed with a lightheart-edness I had never experienced, and that suddenly seemed an intrinsic part of my true self. With that, I was ready to remeet the press.

And once again, the result would be something I couldn't have predicted in a million years.

Chapter 18

Revenge of the Nerd

THINK OF A TIME IN your life when everything felt just right and time just flew by. You could see more clearly, think faster, handle any bump in the road with grace. There wasn't a problem you couldn't solve, a mishap you couldn't bounce back from, a failure you couldn't look in the face and laugh at. You had the energy to do everything you set out to do without tiring from morning to night. You had the sensitivity to smell out an unhealthy person or situation a mile away. You had the gumption to defuse negativity and aggression from others and, having been there, realize they were suffering and offer them empathy. You were the person you always felt you could be, living the life you always wanted.

That was me in the wake of the commercial's incredible success. There was suddenly nothing holding me back, nothing keeping me from accomplishing my bucket list. I was reacting faster, thinking three steps ahead, and discovering ways to bring people together in the pursuit of making the world a better place instead of taking from it. I had become the person I had always wanted to be—not by negating who I was before but by becoming more of myself, letting other parts of my personality emerge, parts I hadn't even known existed.

One such part was an inherent irony, another an innate playfulness. Utterly foreign to me before, both these traits seemed to have been born out of the sense that I had finally beaten and reset the game. I got it. There would never be answers to my existential questions evoked by the inevitability of death. I still knew we were all going to die, but where that thought once drove my life into crisis after crisis, it now took on a fresh meaning seen through my new lenses. Now it meant that since I had nothing to lose, my best option was to have fun within the confines of life's countless contradictions. If nothing really matters, then you can make anything and everything matter. Nonsense makes sense. Nothing has meaning, so therefore just about anything can have meaning; you just have to make it yourself. For once I felt free, no longer bound by the societal pressures that had held me prisoner my whole life.

Serendipitously, this mental metamorphosis came just as the popularity of our commercial had generated a tidal wave of interest from all over the world, eager to take part in the flavor of the moment—Rosenberg and me.

Chantal and I—Rosenberg, too—were flattered beyond belief by all the attention. But having gone through this once before and been burned, we were aware that the specific agenda of the news outlets—to cover the hot story of the moment—was not necessarily in line with *our* agenda. This time, too, knowing the news media needed us and we didn't need them was a blissfully emboldening driving force. Simply put, we had zero intention of playing by their rules but were aware we did need to be in the game.

We knew most of the media outlets after us covered topical entertainment or lighthearted, happy news; it meant if we came out swinging with our message, it would be ignored. What we engineered instead was a compromise of humor, theatrics, and the utmost sincerity—a mix that was, in fact, the perfect extension of who we were.

Ironically, the first time we tried this out was when the stakes were the highest: a live interview on *This Morning*, the United Kingdom's most popular morning show with the usual mix of celebrity interviews, entertainment news, sports, health, cooking, and so on. We did it as a live feed shot directly into the show from a studio in New York City, with the New York skyline visible behind us. Chantal had dressed Rosenberg and me in matching uniforms of the Queen's Guard, the folks who protect Buckingham Palace, complete with humongously high, furry beefeater hats. When the feed cut to us, we both froze as if we were in fact on guard at the Queen's palace. This proved confusing to the hosts and to all the other guests in the room, but we held it for a full minute before I started speaking. I kept this perfectly straight face throughout the interview, mixing humor with straightforward descriptions of the struggles of my life, how Rosenberg had saved me, and how the love of animals could save everyone watching the interview. In order to more closely align with our agenda, I also pointed out that while the British were known for their exemplary teeth, the dental hygiene of their dogs, which I declared should be just as important as their own, tends to be neglected. To emphasize the point, I pulled a toothbrush out of my pocket and began brushing Rosenberg's teeth, offering a demonstration while encouraging viewers to do the same to their pups. Animal gum disease, I exhorted them, can be a big problem that can be easily avoided.

Our second television interview was another morning show, this time Australia's *Sunrise*, which is *that* nation's most popular morning show. This time, Chantal dressed Rosenberg and me in matching Steve Irwin outfits in honor of the late, great Crocodile Hunter, a hero whose mission echoed our own. Our getup included a gigantic stuffed crocodile, fake snakes, and cans of Foster's beer. While being intermittently licked in the face, I explained to the Australian audience my theory about how, amid the exponentially growing instability, contentiousness, and alarming problems in the world, animals can teach us how to solve conflict. Because they don't judge us by how much money we have, whom we vote for, or the color of our skin, animals, I argued, simply treat us as we treat them. For that reason, I went on, talking right over the host attempting to cut me off, Rosenberg and I were campaigning to institute a new position at the United Nations—that of Human-and-Dog Ambassador, a position to which I still aspire to this day.

We did lots of American TV interviews as well—including CNN's *Breaking News*, where Rosenberg and I wore matching sweaters, tweed jackets, and glasses as we debated a notable academic who had written a book explaining why it was wrong to anthropomorphize our dogs. We dressed up as Steve Jobs on Cheddar TV, a livestreamed financial news network, where we were interviewed by hairdresser, activist, and podcaster Jonathan Van Ness about our love for laissez-faire capitalism, the dangers of overconsumption, and our goal of having a positive impact on the world. We donned chef costumes for an appearance on the *Rachael Ray* show, where we campaigned for diversity and world peace. And on *Good Morning America*, wearing matching baby-blue-and-white poodle-patterned shirts, we were honored to share the stage with puppies up for adoption at the North Shore Animal League, whom I petted during the interview while going into detail about how Rosenberg had saved me and how animals bringing out the best in us can help foster world peace.

We rounded out this new batch of publicity with appearances on a bunch of variety shows, game shows, long-form news shows, and podcasts; collaborations with high-fashion clothing brands and animal-centric organizations—our favorites; an appearance at a high school in Alaska, which then asked us to give their commencement address; and an offer from a museum in Quebec that asked to put our likeness in an interactive display—a palette of publicity for our work and, we hoped, for our cause.

The live TV interviews were just about the most fun I had ever had. Surprising myself more than anyone, I not only felt comfortable addressing what I realized were huge audiences, but I also thrived on being a center of attention. Because I didn't know what to expect and had no idea ahead of time what questions I would be asked, I improvised all my answers. Yet what came out struck a chord.

We also started responding to the multitude of interview requests—and requests to use our work—from traditional media and news networks: *New York* magazine, *People*, CBS News, Bravo, *Cosmopolitan*, CNN, *Metro*, *Le Monde* in France, Germany's *Bild*, the *Chosun Ilbo* in South Korea, Mexico's *El Universal*, and the *Sunday Times* of South Africa, plus art magazines and websites all over India, China, Poland, Greece, Brazil, Japan, and other parts of the world.

Predictably, despite the different nations and languages, the questions were pretty much the same, based on the assumption we were novelty-sideshow freaks or emblematic of an American archetype of superficial luxury—symbols of excessive wealth or privilege or the decline of Western civilization, perhaps the decline of the world:

When did you first realize you looked like your dog?

How did you start dressing him up?

Do you have a trust fund or a real job?

How big is the dog's wardrobe?

Do you think dogs are more important than humans?

To avoid being used for anyone else's agenda, we told each outlet we would only conduct interviews or allow access to our work if our answers to their questions were edited *only* for length and appropriateness, not for content. Many outlets said no; full editorial control was their policy. We moved forward only with those that agreed to our demand.

For the publications that consented, I figured out a rope-a-dope system in which, as on the talk shows, I would answer part of the question, then catch the questioner off guard by weaving in some self-referential absurdist humor before unloading what I really wanted to say: dogs can make us better people and help us shape a better world.

At this point in my saga, such statements flowed out of me instinctively and with overwhelming force. Most came to me as I spoke and were fleshed out over time, becoming the guiding principles of what I consider my life's work, the same principles that inspired me to write this book. Expressed at first in varying ways, refined across different formats, then translated into different languages (thanks, Google Translate), these principles came together in a clear and concise format I call the Dog Dad Manifesto, and to find it, all you have to do is turn the page.

Chapter 19

The Dog Dad Manifesto

HUMAN SURVIVAL AND THE EVENTUAL dominance of humans over competing humanoid species most likely would not have happened without the help and partnership of dogs. The canines of the past acted as our hunting partners, protectors, and transporters. Eons later, today, a different kind of survival is in question—humanity's exponentially increasing existential crisis—and once again, canines may well function as our healers. The sheer number of dogs in the lives of the human population is numeric proof of their popularity, but our lack of understanding of how and why we are drawn to and depend on these animals prevents us from taking advantage of their magic in many ways. Why? That's the question my manifesto answers.

Dogs can bring us into harmony with nature at a time of environmental peril. The exponentially accelerating global climate change will be the greatest threat to humans since our early existence. It derives from our disregard and abusive behavior, a result of the supreme human folly of believing we are above nature, not a part of it. When we are free-falling toward ultimate destruction, it is paramount that we accept our place in the natural world. Our dogs, as evolutionary partners and certified members of the natural world, are our closest portal to that world. They don't eat more than they need, nor do they destroy their surroundings and pollute air and water needed by other creatures. They live in harmony with the natural world and, as our best friends, provide the perfect example of how we should be handling ourselves.

Dogs give us the gift of innocence. We are all born pure and innocent. We lose both inherent characteristics the moment we are able to intentionally commit sin and are figuratively banished from "the garden"—the paradise of Eden or a similar place of guiltlessness. Whether we are aware of it or not, we all forever long to regain the innocence of this paradise and escape from the harsh realities of our cruel world. All animals—but in particular dogs, the closest friends of our species—perpetually live in the garden. While we humans are never quite able to return to it, we channel the garden through the osmosis gained in our close proximity to dogs. This alone can explain both our magnetic attachment to dogs and their otherworldly, alchemical effect on us.

Dogs remind us of the importance of play. While play is a principal priority when we're first discovering the world, as we're weathered by its realities and we become driven by productivity, our outlook on life becomes less whimsical. While it may seem trivial, there are tremendous downsides to this. Playing helps us improve bonds, stimulate creativity, stay feeling youthful and energetic, and release endorphins and thus de-stress. Pups never lose their waggish mindset, though, or their sense of humor, a contagious mood booster for us.

Dogs live in the moment. In the age of technology, perhaps our greatest vices are our short attention spans, the impulse to multitask, the incessant desire for something more or something different, the obsession with productivity. The result? We seldom live in the moment; we are rarely capable of being present. Our dogs, by contrast, are never too busy to interact with us and consistently urge us to stop overcomplicating our lives and take them for a walk or play with them instead. Dogs also—and this is very tough for me to think about—have drastically shorter life spans than us. This should remind us to be present, to make every moment count, and to enjoy ourselves rather than worry about the past or the future, as our oversize, overcomplicated brains and conflicting emotions often drive us to do. This "presentness" is what drives us to happiness, the natural state of both dogs and humans. The incessant excitability of dogs, their eye contact, tail-wagging, face-licking, and unparalleled bliss in our company are constant reminders for us to be happy with who we are, what we have, and the fact that we're alive—facts we all too often lose sight of or just plain forget.

Dogs can bring people together. All humans, even proud introverts like me, are social creatures. Isolation is unhealthy for us—emotionally, mentally, and physically. Spending too much time alone almost literally invites the risk of mood instability, general unhappiness, even mental illness. Because we evolved with dogs—and as a result, are born with a magnetism toward them—having a dog attracts other humans, which in turn encourages social interaction, affability, and friendship itself. We see this every time we take our pups for a walk, which is perhaps the most instinctual social contract in human evolution. The human-and-dog linkage across a leash or at opposite ends of a game of fetch ignites vast opportunities for social interaction. Strangers are prompted to react, converse, relate as fellow dog-loving friends. Stunningly, this ability—the power dogs possess to bring us together—still remains a font of tremendous, untapped potential.

Dogs bring out our empathy, no matter how deeply it is buried. One of the defining traits of us humans is our capacity for empathy. Life's tribulations may prompt us to grow a shell around our feelings so that, for sheer self-preservation, we bury some of the kindness born of the innocence we once possessed, lose touch with our emotions, even become dysfunctional. But being around the vulnerability of dogs, who depend on our love and care to survive, can open a portal back to the reserves of empathy within us, and caring for a dog can rebuild this path until empathy is once again our default.

To test the truth of this, think about someone you dislike or who makes you uncomfortable—maybe even scares you. Now picture that person petting a dog, caring for a dog. It diminishes your animosity, doesn't it?

It also reminds us of the necessity, shared by humans and dogs, to touch and be touched. Just petting a dog's head, not to mention getting licked by a pup, literally stimulates the release of oxytocin, the pleasure and relaxation hormone that lowers heart rate and blood pressure, reduces stress, and promotes our relaxation—proof that dogs make us feel happy and thus bring out our empathy.

Dogs strengthen our ability to love. Love, the strongest and most infectious life force in the universe, is the power that connects all sentient and perhaps insentient beings. We humans certainly possess the capacity for love, which we keep figuratively harnessed in what I'll call a love generator. Over time, thanks to the complexities of life and the harsh realities of the world, these generators malfunction or become depleted. Dogs, who love unconditionally, act as love batteries. Their loyalty, nobility, and innocence, which sometimes feel like the only purity and goodness remaining in the world, renew our faith, and that in turn jump-starts our depleted generators, powering us once again to love and emit our own light.

Dogs know how to forgive. Forgiveness is something humans are not good at. Fueled by our egos and our most double-sided emotion, pride, we have a tendency to take things personally and hold grudges. These spiteful feelings start small but can grow into hate, which can spark much larger conflicts—even war. By contrast, because dogs live in the present, they let go of their anger fast enough that it never has a chance to fester. Every minute, every hour, every day becomes a fresh start, and with every fresh start, dogs absolve themselves and everyone else of residual anger. Instead, they are ready to face-lick their human nonstop and flash that canine Kool-Aid smile while running at top speed after a tennis ball. If humans did this, it would dramatically reduce conflict in our personal and professional lives, while at the same time reduce interpersonal and international conflicts, thus improving and benefiting the entire world.

Loving dogs is universal. Dog people span every race, religion, creed, nationality, and socioeconomic background. Everyone's dogs are monumentally important to their lives, and this commitment is, with certainty, one thing they can all agree on. What if the world could harness this potential as a unifying bridge across which even the most loathsome of enemies might meet to overcome their mutual animosity, their prejudices, their perceived differences, and unite in the worship they share of this entirely different species? If enemies could only see the love of dogs in each other, might this not prove that there is good in everyone, and might that not be the link that ends the enmity? Worth a try, no?

Dogs exemplify humility. Ego just might be the most dangerous part of our personalities. Too much of it can breed arrogance, narcissism, self-centeredness, and entitlement—all qualities that can lead to unhappiness for us and negativity toward others. Our dogs, by contrast, have no concept of ego. In fact, they spend every second of their waking lives unaffected by notions of success, remaining as down-to-earth and approachable as the day they were born. They serve as humility reminders, personifying such acts as admitting when we don't know something—or in my case, admitting when I am wrong—acting without ego, and accepting help from others. Simply put, dogs embody humility, a trait that has the power to break down barriers, connect with others, and bring the greatest happiness and harmony into our lives.

Dogs are family. Perhaps the most succinct and important tenet of The Dog Dad Manifesto, based in a truth that encompasses all the others, is this one: dogs are family. In the dawn of time, they helped our species flourish, taught us the art of survival, helped us heal the wounds of the human condition, and served as our children and best friends. They deserve to be universally respected and indeed revered, put on a pedestal and treated as we wish to be treated by others.

Sadly, while there are billions of us who adore our dogs, there are also billions who mistreat, abuse, and even consume these best friends. To me these are heinous crimes, and we can counter them in many institutional and individual ways. But I believe we should start with language. So this manifesto proposes that we do away with the word "pet," which seems to me derogatory, implying subservience and objectification. That's a bad fit for creatures that act as our emotional guides, teaching us about empathy, loyalty, unconditional love, forgiveness, respect for our environment, how to be present, and how to become better versions of ourselves.

Instead, how about referring to our pups as "kids," "fur children," or—for anyone worried about sounding strange—"animal companions"? Family isn't defined solely by blood or by specific roles, but by caring, companionship, and, above all else, love. If you take nothing else away from this book or The Dog Dad Manifesto, know this: embracing the truth that dogs are family can bring out the best in us and *will* help save the world.

Chapter 20

"Only 'Roommate Issues'"

EARLIER IN THIS BOOK, I wrote—at some length—about my difficulties as a young person who suffered from social anxiety, about how hard it was for me to express my feelings and articulate my emotions. Tongue-tied at best, dumbstruck at worst, I found it virtually impossible to sustain any relationship with depth or substance. The void this created generated an all-consuming need for intimacy, a condition, as I would later learn in therapy, known as autophobia—the fear of being alone forever. Ashamed of this hunger, I kept it a secret and tucked it away deep down inside, until it was uncovered by my heroic cognitive shrink.

I remember the moment perfectly, though it is now years ago. I was sitting on a worn-out leather couch in the parlor of an Upper West Side brownstone. Outside, it was raining hard, which somehow added a dankness I could almost taste in the air. My shrink proposed I ask him questions about dating.

"How will I know?" I asked him. "How I will recognize the person who is right for me—who is the 'one'?"

His answer struck me as disturbingly unromantic. "You'll know when the problems between you two are neither big nor serious. When the difficulties are at most just roommate issues, you'll know the two of you are right for each other."

By "roommate issues" he meant things like one of you not washing the dishes after a meal or someone neglecting to put the toilet seat down—stuff like that. In his theory, couples who contend over issues bigger than these roommate issues are pretty much doomed. The reason: despite wanting to change their ways, most people simply don't have the capacity to do so—not by much, anyway.

I had next to no experience in relationships, so I couldn't really argue the point, though from what I had witnessed of relationships— my parents, my few friends, couples on TV and in movies—big fights did not seem uncommon. It wasn't until I met and fell in love with Chantal that I realized my shrink's theory finally made perfect sense.

From the second we met, the very instant Rosenberg and I fell in love with her, with the exception of our first phone call or two, the interactions between Chantal and me felt completely natural. As a person accustomed to keeping a package of canned subjects on hand for small talk, this was revolutionary. Our chemistry was instantaneous, though entirely platonic at first, and while it took a few months for Chantal to reciprocate my love, once she did, everything just clicked, organically falling into just the right place.

When her apartment lease expired, she moved in with me, a decision that barely required a conversation, as I couldn't have waited any longer.

To say that Rosenberg became obsessed with Chantal would be a gargantuan understatement; they were instantly inseparable. As I watched their relationship blossom, and as I saw the love she gave him, which was different from the love I gave him, I felt no jealousy. In fact, as a guy who is passionate about his pack, I felt more joy than I could have ever imagined. Before we knew it, Rosenberg, too, only reached his peak level of happiness when the three of us were together, and that thrilled me. He began to refuse to eat unless all three of us were present and started running to the "missing" other at top speed when we came home, barking, jumping, and licking profusely.

This habit, which became solidified behavior after our second round of dealing with the press, is what I employed to surprise Chantal with something special.

It was a normal Saturday morning. Rosenberg and I went out for a walk, giving Chantal time and space in which she could light jasmine-scented candles for a long bath and just be by herself. Rosenberg and I visited the dog park, where he caught up with his friends, then stopped in our favorite coffee shop on the way home. I sat down at a somewhat crowded table then pulled out from my jacket pocket a wedding ring, a crumpled paper bag, and some twine. I put the ring in the bag, folded it several times, tied it with the yarn, and fastened it to Rosenberg's harness.

As my son and I proceeded home, my heart started to race, my armpits began to sweat, and my breathing quickened. I chalked it up to half positive anxiety, half fear of being rejected, which would then send me into the deepest, darkest emotional hell any person who had ever lived had ever known.

But with Rosenberg as my safety net by my side, I picked him up, despite now dripping with sweat, and soldiered on. The second we opened the door and I put him down, as predicted, he ran to Chantal at full speed as if his life depended on it. He jumped onto her, and she immediately saw the string of yarn and the thing it was attached to on his harness. For a moment, she seemed perplexed, then she took hold of the paper bag and opened it, looked at me with a humongous smile, grabbed my head, kissed me, and said, "I love you, and yes, I do."

Intoxicated by the high we felt, we saw the occasion as an opportunity to create an atmosphere that would be an extension of us and that would bring pleasure to others. Happily, the money we saved from the Sprint commercial enabled us to fulfill our outlandish dreams for our wedding.

Of course we invited our families—all the people and animal companions we treasured in our lives. Kids were discouraged but not unwelcome, and dogs were mandatory.

On a late summer day, we all descended upon an idyllic, animal-friendly hotel in a rural area near Woodstock. A rescue-farm petting zoo was set up adjacent to the aisle, and there, beautiful llamas, alpacas, baby foxes, mini horses, sheep, goats, and pigs all nibbled on their flower necklaces. Chantal and I played with every one of these animals, but we took even greater joy in watching our friends and family smile from ear to ear, transfixed with happiness and channeling their innocence—a treasure trove of delight captured in photograph after photograph.

Ja Rule and Ashanti's "Always on Time" announced it was time for the ceremony. Holding Rosenberg in my arms—we wore matching black suits—I walked down the aisle with my parents, while Chantal walked with her mother and an alpaca, who had become her fast friend. A simple altar made of birchwood was topped with a white canopy that matched Chantal's multilayered, wraparound Zimmerman dress. The officiant, our closest mutual friend, Béat Baudendorfer, at our request wore a grass-green, full-body cloak reminiscent of the elven and hobbit cloaks worn in *The Lord of the Rings*. Since Béat is Liechtensteinian, we asked him to speak in his native dialect, which we thought was interesting and which added a fun aura of mystery to the moment. When the time for the actual vows arrived, instead of reciting them aloud, we whispered gibberish to each other, then in turn stuck our tongues in each other's ears.

Later that evening, there were speeches—delivered first by my parents, then by my oldest friends, Dante and Adam, who both talked a lot about my past, then highlighted my recent metamorphosis, which both attributed to Chantal. When it was time for me to speak, I was characteristically scared senseless, but taking in the happy faces of people I loved around me soothed my nerves. Without hesitation, I got up, stood tall, smiled widely, and let my improvisational words gush out.

"Human and animal family and friends, we are so grateful you joined us to celebrate this joyous occasion, which is already the best day of my life—thank you! I'd also like to thank our son, who is my best man—" I turned to the right and looked down at him sitting on Chantal's lap, where he barked as if on cue.

Then I looked up into Chantal's already tear-filled eyes and began to address my bride. "Chantal, a.k.a. Minky, Binky, Rainbow Princess, Mother of Poodles." I stopped and half smirked. "Because I was always odd, off, and even unrelatable before you, I had given up on the idea I would have a human life partner. But when I learned about you, first through your work, I felt a magnet pulling me toward you. So I figured out which park you frequented"—my voice cracked a little—"and went there every day, which in retrospect, is creepy and could be considered stalking. From the day we met, I knew I had finally found another person from my home planet. I knew this because you instantly accepted me and brought out the best in me. Soon after, I was in love and would learn you were the most kindhearted, optimistic, badass, brilliant *Homo sapiens* I had ever known. Every day you teach me that anything is possible and the hardest situations can even be harnessed into having the most fun. Being close to your humongous heart, eternal integrity, and benevolent nature helps make me the best person I can be, the person I am the proudest to be.

"Because nothing in life is easy, I know our journey together won't always be. With our future horde of human and animal kids will come calamities, which will inevitably give us wrinkles we'll pretend are laugh lines and hair that turns even more gray. But no matter how decrepit we become, and no matter what happens, like today, we'll always find a way to make life feel like a fantasy. And until the final day when one of us passes, we'll always be the two clowns who not only run but literally own the circus."

I looked at Chantal as she burst into happy tears and stood up, with Rosenberg in her arms, then kissed me hard on the lips before motioning for the mic. I handed it to her then sat down.

In contrast to my long-windedness, she succinctly said, "Topher, I am the luckiest woman in the world. I love you so much, am so happy, and have such joyous feelings they can't accurately be put into words. I love everyone here, and thank you for welcoming us as a couple and all being an important part of our happy family."

The rest of the wedding felt like I was living in a fantasy. Having everyone I loved from every stage of my life together and celebrating, to this day, was the most blissful sequence of events I've ever experienced and marked yet another milestone: I became an emotionally complete, full-fledged person who was able to—and deserved to—experience happiness. I had become the person I had forever wished to be.

Chapter 21

Behemoth-Sized Bombshell

ASIDE FROM THE HARROWING INEVITABLY that we will all die, the biggest burden humans carry is that despite how good things are going, an accident, ailment, act of God, or other catastrophe beyond our control can derail our lives any time. It is when we are experiencing our highest moments that we are at our most vulnerable because it is almost unimaginable for us to obsess over a calamity lurking around the corner. And no matter what we've achieved or think we understand, something will always come along and blindside us, most often when we least expect it.

After the wedding, we did what just about every other newlywed couple does and can attest to—we resumed our normal lives. A mini honeymoon at our favorite off-leash dog-friendly Amagansett beach found us coming up with all sorts of new ideas, concepts, and strategies, and feeling collectively introspective and inspired, the three of us got to work, shooting photos and writing pensive paragraphs to accompany them. We were back in full execution mode.

To counter what we deemed to be unhealthy notions about body image and beauty standards, we enlisted a friend who has alopecia, wanting to pair her with a hairless dog and dress them both in "Bald Is Beautiful" T-shirts. But our friend protested! She refused to be seen with the hairless dog, whom she considered "gross," so instead we shot a photo with just her and us—that is, Rosenberg and me—which ended up being reposted on blogs all over the world.

We also shot concept photos to raise money for victims of natural catastrophes and for promoting trans rights. And joining the fight for animal protection legislation all over the world, we dressed as judges, complete with judicial robes and British barrister wigs, and held gavels up high to raise money for the Animal Legal Defense Fund.

We started shooting more TV news segments as well. For a show in France, we dressed up as artists, wearing berets, of course, and surrounded by fifty baguettes (which we donated to a homeless shelter afterward). For the sister show in Germany, we wore lederhosen in humble homage to Oktoberfest.

Rounding out our postwedding frenzy, we set out to combat the growing epidemic of obesity. Chantal dressed us up as various fruits and veggies, and we walked around different supermarkets, interacting with totally perplexed people, to discourage the consumption of refined sugar and to promote cardiovascular health.

In a particularly apt demonstration of irony, toward the end of this health-promoting "fruit shoot," Chantal, who is indecently filled with boundless energy, suddenly began feeling startlingly, debilitatingly lethargic—*despite* getting more than her fair share of sleep. This would turn out to be symptomatic of something not just unexpected but, once again, life-changing for both of us.

As the days went by and Chantal's lethargy continued—and in fact increased—I found it highly disturbing. But since her yearly physical with her primary care doctor was—fortuitously!—due to take place the next week, and since she remained in good spirits, she decided to wait until that appointment for a "diagnosis" rather than get herself checked out sooner.

Any anxiety-prone person like me—and particularly one with all my health issues—will easily understand how my mind responded to this delay, imagining all the worst-case scenarios. Nevertheless, I didn't want to cause Chantal any unnecessary stress, so I kept these imaginings to myself. We just continued on as normal, which, among other things, meant planning our next shoot, a video set in medieval times and aimed at showing how hard life was back then so as to encourage people to appreciate being born in the present.

Since Chantal wasn't really up to it, I took on the role of prepping the shoot and finding and obtaining the right costumes and props. That is why, on the very day of Chantal's appointment with her doctor, Rosenberg and I headed into Manhattan to visit our favorite costume shop, Abracadabra. This store boasts a professional-level rental section in its discombobulated, sweaty basement that is also home to an oversize tabby cat named Floppy, who is called that because his tongue flops sideways out of his mouth. I loved Floppy.

We walked there from Brooklyn—a long trek, all the way over the Williamsburg Bridge and then some—so I was already perspiring when we arrived. By the time I had managed, in the constricted space of the mothball-scented dressing room, to put on all seven pieces of the King Henry VIII costume, sweat was pouring down from my forehead on both sides of my nose. Just as I was about to swipe a rivulet from my face, Chantal phoned.

I answered in a banal tone.

She said she had important news that she preferred to tell me in person, so she asked us to meet her at home in an hour. I pleaded for her to tell me more, but she refused. Assuming the possibility that she had just received devastating news, I decided not to push any further. But I could feel my heart rate ratcheting up, and now dripping with snowballing sweat, I began to take off what felt like ten pounds of buffoonish costume clothing, layer by layer. Halfway through, I looked down at Rosenberg, also panting with anxiety and with a nonplussed expression on his face as he watched my shenanigans from the floor.

The subway ride home took a total of twenty-five minutes but may as well have been the longest ride of my life. Luckily, we found a seat, which was crucial because I felt so lightheaded, I'm not sure I would have been able to stand up and hold onto Rosenberg, whose feet I never allow to touch a subway floor. With him safely on my lap, my mind raced through a range of doomsday scenarios, each one adding to the sweat now cascading down my chest and lower back and, I was sure, forming puddles around my seat. I tried analyzing the tone in which she had delivered her message; it had been decidedly neutral. I reviewed everything she had said, but this just compounded the mystery. My conclusion was that it was a big diagnosis that would require a specialist, so she would inevitably need further examination. So maybe it was a fluke, maybe it was a misdiagnosis.

But I knew cancer ran in her family, so maybe the doctor identified a lump in her breast or a dark spot on her brain. I knew pancreatic cancer was on the rise, so maybe this might be the problem, but that was unlikely since pancreatic cancer ran in my family, not hers. A friend of a friend had recently been diagnosed with muscular dystrophy, which never gets better; maybe this was what the doctor found. Maybe, I thought, it was something intimate or embarrassing—a female problem or gallbladder or kidney stones—none a big deal but not the sort of thing to announce in public in case there were people next to her when she phoned me.

That whole subway ride, my mind kept racing, and my stomach kept tying itself in ever-tighter knots as I sat squished between two Hasidic Jewish men, neither of whom seemed thrilled at being so close to Rosenberg, despite my assuring them he was Jewish *and* circumcised, just like them. I closed my eyes, trying to calm myself down, and saw faint kaleidoscopic patterns, likely the result of the industrial tungsten lights my eyes couldn't escape. In that moment I acknowledged how dreamlike the past months had been and concluded that inevitably the luck had to run out. My lifelong habit of self-sabotage kicked right back in, and muscle memory reactivated all the old thoughts: what a fool I was to even think I could be happy! And having thought it, I would now have to accept the awful fate that awaited me as punishing karma. Our relationship was too good to be true. Chantal, and with her all my happiness, would be taken away from me.

Strange noises prompted me to open my eyes for a second, and I noticed a group of high school kids sitting across from me, pointing, laughing, and staring, either because they recognized Rosenberg or because I was sweating so profusely. Now even deeper into a torturous hell, I closed my eyes again and focused my attention on stroking Rosenberg's velvety head to help hold myself together.

Suddenly, we arrived at our stop, and I jumped up, Rosenberg still in my arms. That's when I noticed the sweat marks I had left on the seat, and at once, the old, familiar feelings of humiliation, shame, and self-disgust washed over me. This was it. This was the end.

I walked into the apartment and was immediately hit with the scent of Chantal's favorite jasmine candle, so I knew she was already home. Despite the torture I had put myself through, I certainly did not want to put any extra burden on her, so as I took off Rosenberg's leash, then my shoes, I put on a happy face and walked to the other side of the apartment to greet her.

Per usual, however, Rosenberg, once released, darted to her and barked his typically needful bark until she picked him up and let him lick her face. Then, even before kissing me hello, she invited me to sit with her on the couch, which seemed to me uncharacteristically formal. I nevertheless mustered every ounce of self-control possible, sat down as instructed, and remained quiet, though my right hand nervously pinched the couch's gray-blue corduroy fabric in a Tourette-like tick.

Before saying a word, she looked me dead in the eye with a stern, straight face. Then she began to speak, and my eyes seemed transfixed on reading her lips so I could hear the words a millisecond or two sooner and understand at once. My heart was beating out of my chest; sweat, of course, was coming out of every pore of my body; and my stomach was doing slow-motion summersaults. I was able to make out only three words, which couldn't have been any more unexpected nor could they have made any less sense. "I am repugnant," Chantal announced.

I gasped. Loudly. "Huh! What?"

She said it again, but this time I forced myself to close my eyes so as to listen with my ears only. "I said I'm pregnant."

Total shock—plus monumental relief.

My face froze for a moment, and I saw hers scrunch up. That's when the flood began.

I burst into tears from a kind of happiness I could barely comprehend. I hugged and kissed her with an overexcitement I assumed occurred only in the movies. Rosenberg jumped up from the floor onto the couch and started licking the happy tears off my face, then turned to licking Chantal. With our brains short-circuiting from shock, extreme jubilation, positively overwhelming anxiety, and disbelief, we sat on the couch, processing the medley of emotions that are inescapable for parents-to-be who have just discovered their lives are about to change.

While there were so many things I couldn't know, there were a few things I had zero ambiguity about: How much I loved Chantal. How much I loved Rosenberg. How I knew that, as a family, we would stop at nothing to be the best parents in the world. And how that would mean treating our human and animal children equally and, through our work and our parenting, creating a positive impact on everyone around us, using whatever powers we have, in the midst of whatever chaos might loom.

Chapter 22

Humans, Too, Are Nature

THE HUMAN SPECIES IS KNOWN officially and scientifically as *Homo sapiens sapiens*. *Sapiens* comes from the Latin word *sapientia*, which means wisdom. It is worth noting that it was humans who gave us that name, denoting us *twice* as wise, probably because we were clever enough to build shelters, live in cities, and catalog everything into distinctive categories.

But humans are not always all that bright, and at the heart of human idiocy is our collective denial of the fact that we are part of the animal kingdom, a denial that keeps us stumbling around under the false notion that we are actually *above* animals. Given the behaviors we undeniably share with our animal ancestors—birth and death, the need for nourishment and eliminating waste—not to mention the fossil evidence of our evolution, the denial of our animal connection is clearly another result of the conflict between our instincts and our rational minds.

Among these shared instinctual processes, one in particular, in my view, delivers the coup de grâce to both creationists and the so-called human nature deniers. I mean, of course, what our parents went through to bring us into this world, the exact thing Chantal and I faced at this moment in our story: pregnancy and childbirth. The mind-bending experience of bringing a new life into this world is the best example of our own mortality; it also cements into every parent our place in the natural world. How it does not simultaneously produce an existential crisis in every parent-to-be will always be beyond me.

Already prone to bouts of angst, my brain, as the pregnancy unfolded, naturally jumped into hyperdrive. I began asking myself a range of questions: Am I worthy of being a human father? Am I up to the challenge? Am I healthy enough emotionally to shepherd a human life into this world? Or am I still too selfish and narcissistic to do the job? And with overpopulation and an astonishing environmental catastrophe looming, is bringing onto the planet another human who will use up dwindling resources even the responsible thing to do?

Will having a child interfere with or undermine our relationship with Rosenberg? This question—and the fear it represented—gave me perhaps the most worry. I had heard about people who discard their animal children when a human baby arrives. The mere thought fills me with almost uncontrollable anger approaching serious rage because I knew with every cell in my body that Chantal and I would never ever act in that way. But how many other people have made that same vow?

And what if Rosenberg—and this was so uncharacteristic of him as to be silly—but *what if* he became jealous and attacked the baby? Would the police force us to give him up? Would Chantal, Rosenberg, the baby, and I be forced to put on disguises (Rosenberg and I had plenty) and go on the run, fleeing the state, exiling ourselves from the country? We were prepared to do all of that should push come to shove.

There were so many questions I could not answer, but I did know Chantal was—and still is—a kindhearted, nurturing, generous, responsible, loving person, the ideal life partner. Whatever my shortcomings—and they are numerous—I knew she would rise to any occasion and, if need be, prop me up. She, Rosenberg, and I were soul mates who loved each other deeply. Therefore, no matter what adversities we faced as individuals or as a collective unit, we would act with honor, integrity, morality, and empathy.

While I spent time wrestling with these thoughts, my dear wife was wrestling with the unfathomable discomfort of the later stages of pregnancy, a discomfort that became more unbearable by the day. With what her doctor described as an "extra-large" belly, along with the normal hormonal shifts and bodily disruptions, not to mention a colossal lack of sleep—this alone would have driven me to insanity—she was as vulnerable and as restless as I'd ever seen her. As her seemingly countless symptoms grew worse, I transitioned into a full-time cook, cleaner, masseur, butler, and emotional support person—all of which provided me with something proactive to do and distracted me from my mounting worries.

Despite this and my gallant efforts, I was powerless to alleviate her suffering. Thankfully, though, where I failed, Rosenberg—the alchemist, the fluffy love battery, powered by the sheer divinity of his species—succeeded. Like his angelically fanged brethren who can gauge the state of their humans and adjust their care accordingly, Rosenberg sensed the changes Chantal was experiencing and adapted his behavior, kicking his nurturing and protective tendencies into a higher gear. Once glued to me, he transitioned to be permanently either at Chantal's side or seated in a defensive position near the doors. When she was in bed at her worst moments, a state of affairs that caused me nervously and helplessly to pace back and forth, I'd look back, mystified, to see her suddenly smiling from ear to ear, stroking Rosenberg's face as he licked her and calling him the many nicknames she had come up with: Poodlefresh, Poodle Slim, Baby Afghan, Tenured Professor Wigglebottoms, Petite Brad Pitt, Brown Bomber, What Can Brown Do for You?, and perhaps my two most commonly used, Little Paw and Little Owl.

Her escalating discomfort, however, made it increasingly more difficult—and eventually impossible—for us to do our work. She was, after all, our photographer, videographer, lighting expert, stylist, prop master, and creative director, and much as she wanted to continue to do it all, it became clearer with every passing day that she needed to rest.

The solution, which was also a healthy distraction for Chantal, was to have her order me around, in effect teaching me to perform all her roles. May I say: it was extraordinarily challenging work!

We also determined that she should get in front of the camera, an ideal way to empathize with others going through the same discomforts of pregnancy. Ever the creative artist, she found ways to use her huge baby bump in costumes—as Violet Beauregarde from Willy Wonka, next to me as the namesake role and Rosenberg as an Oompa Loompa, and as Mother Earth, days away from giving birth—which to this day are among our most popular posts.

Yes, our output slowed down temporarily, but we still received numerous emails about our work every day from various sources. One email came from an awards show called the Shorty Awards, and it informed us that we had been nominated for the show's Instagrammer of the Year award. Clueless as to what this meant, we replied that we were flattered but, with a baby on the way, even on the off chance we might win, it wouldn't be possible for us to attend and personally collect the award.

This prompted a phone call from a very nice woman assuring us that even being in the running for the award was a major achievement and asking if there was any way we could reconsider. We could only reply that, as parents-to-be who had no control over our baby's timing, our focus was on the present, and while we were honored by the recognition, we could make no promises until after the baby arrived.

It was all a really nice ego boost at a stressful time when it was particularly welcome, but we put it behind us and went back to the waiting game.

And waited.

And waited.

And waited…until the due date came and went.

Then we waited some more until, finally, the time came.

After a not dangerous but difficult pregnancy, Chantal underwent an uncharacteristically complication-free, storybook birth, one that our doctor, a close friend to this day, described as being "fit for a princess." She delivered a perfect little boy whom—for the first and only time I'll break my humility rule and brag—multiple nurses described as "the most beautiful newborn they had ever seen." As a family that loves alliteration, we named him Topper Tinsley.

As every parent can attest, witnessing the birth of your child is the most mind-blowing, happiest, and transformative highlight life can offer. No matter how many classes we take, how many books we read, or how many informative videos we watch, nothing adequately prepares us for this experience, the epicenter of what it is to be human, which clarifies the very concept of existence itself. While I can't cite empirical proof, I am convinced that apart from the more obvious, superficial reasons for this, what makes the arrival of progeny so clarifying is that it ignites one of the purest forms of instinct over logic, revealing to us with shattering coherence that we have acted solely and purely like the animals we are and are doing exactly what we are made to do: procreate.

The birth of a child also totally thwarts our notions of control, predictability, and planning—particularly for the type As among us, who revel in keeping control over almost every aspect of our lives. In the final days of this process, with nature in the driver's seat, planning flies out the window. And as in all matters of life, the unknown looms—a parent's worst nightmare, the dreaded notion of a dangerous complication or undetected defect—both possible outcomes in what is, after all, a high-risk activity. So, aware of the incomprehensible disaster we had just dodged, we reveled in the joy and will never forget our good luck.

There are some people, though (Chantal is one of them), who can and do create plans that will cover almost all bases—the foreseen and the unforeseen—in order to hedge what seems like every bet. It is why, in handling the logistics of the birth, she alerted her sister to remain on standby, ready to rush Rosenberg to the hospital and into our room just minutes after Topper Tinsley was born. Rosenberg, charmingly and festively curious, immediately began to sniff his newborn baby brother, after which he attempted to lick him, thereby confirming his approval. He then parked himself under Topper Tinsley's bassinet on top of a swaddle that carried the baby's smell, clearly and appropriately ready to guard him as if Topper Tinsley were his own.

Now reunited, and despite Chantal's exhausted state, my superhuman wife disclosed to me a hilarious special plan she was ready to enact. She revealed that in addition to the normal contents of the prestocked hospital bag—food, drinks, books, pillows, diapers—she had, unbeknownst to me, packed doctors' scrubs and stethoscopes for Rosenberg and me. She wanted to create a photo that would suggest Rosenberg had been in the delivery room for the actual birth. So just hours after her labor, directing the shoot from her hospital bed, Chantal ordered us to put on our outfits and prepare for action. With her sister behind the camera, it took just one shot to hit the perfect pose.

To this day that photo is and will forever be our favorite, not only for its zaniness and delight, but because it will stand forever as ironclad proof that no matter what changes we may go through, Rosenberg will forever be at the center of our lives, affirming our sacred oath that his role in our home will never be diminished—and that dogs are family.

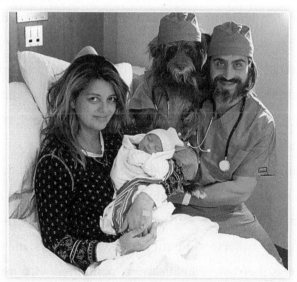

As most first-time parents would agree, despite the fact that humans have been having babies for some two hundred thousand years, and despite what they teach you in the hospital, and despite hours of intense prior preparation, when you get home, it feels like you have no idea what you are doing. Since babies don't come with a manual, we learn the basics and the specifics through trial and error—like any rookie—and despite the disorienting lack of sleep, we eventually find a rhythm and discover what makes our neonates most comfortable.

With Topper Tinsley, perhaps our first breakthrough was discovering that if he continued crying despite having had plenty of sleep, nourishment, and cleaning attention, it was likely because he was bored. We remedied this by continually changing his environment, by letting him touch different textures, and by keeping him constantly in motion. What also helped tremendously was that, even as a newborn baby, he was transfixed by Rosenberg, and the feeling was mutual. We did regulate Rosenberg's desire to lick Topper Tinsley steadily and at all times, but we also encouraged the two of them to interact under careful supervision. And for me witnessing this was an experience I can only describe as blissful, enlightening, and transforming.

Certainly, I had met human babies in the past, but having one of my own made me realize I had never truly interacted with a brand-new human being. Aside from how amazing newborns smell and how adorably otherworldly they look, what struck me like a thunderbolt was their sheer helplessness combined with pure, unadulterated, blissful innocence. To me Topper Tinsley was the epitome of innocence, the kind of innocence I was thinking of when I first learned the definition of the word in my childhood. Back then it made me think of Bambi. Cementing this further were his ginormous anime eyes, which he inherited from his mother and which seemed to cover an adorably disproportionate amount of his face. Unlike me but just like his furry brother, Topper Tinsley had absolutely zero conception of his existence, and his tiny feet, which were smaller than my thumbs, like his brother's paws, stayed firmly in "the garden."

So despite the delirium I was experiencing from the sheer intoxication of being a *human* father for the first time, witnessing the interactions between my two pure sons seemed to pump up my serotonin into what was yet another new high for me. Whatever nefariousness was at work in the world could be washed away by their example of innocence. Now, innocence upon innocence raised that power to the nth possible degree. These two beings—one human, one canine—unable to do anything involving premeditation, born as different species and now at different life stages, were in fact exactly the same. This realization may be obvious to others, but to me, it was revolutionary. It was proof that as humans, no matter what life serves us and what monsters some of us become, we are all born inherently good, and this realization alone seemed to me further proof of how possible it is to take back our purity and goodness once we lose it.

This insight provided me with a newfound elation and brought me a sense of optimism rooted in satisfaction about our species and hope for the world. I sensed that as I continued to witness the phenomenon, it would fuel the evolution of our work. All we needed now was precisely the one thing we would not get for a long time: sleep.

Chapter 23

All Too Human

FRIEDRICH NIETZSCHE (1844-1900) WAS A brilliant philosopher, scholar, poet, you-name-it whose writings have had a profound influence on the intellectual history of the world. When I was a troubled young man in college, I read his work for the first time and found myself intrigued by his idea of the exemplary, superior man of the future—the ideal human who could rise above conventional morality to create and impose his own values. Already isolated because of the mental baggage I carried, my overall anxiety, and just because I was a young putz, I was captivated by that notion and thought I'd like to become one of those men one day. The word Nietzsche used for it was *Übermensch*, German for "superman."

By the way, Nietzsche went nuts at the age of forty-four and died not long after. But that didn't stop me. I was still attracted to the idea that I might possess the internal creative power to live by my own rules, follow my own norms, set my own moral guides. I would not be pushed around like a rag doll by the changing whims and disposable trends of society at large. What kept me from becoming that superman, though, was a big impediment called "life." It turns out that I shared with all those other lower beings around me a certain number of basic needs: food, water, clothing, sleep, shelter. It's hard to rise above any of those needs, much less to fulfill them, without dealing on a practical level with a lot of other humans.

Let's face it, we humans are pack animals. We live and hunt in a herd—for some, maybe in a smallish clique; for most, in a crowd. So how we interact with and are perceived by others is hardwired into us and our happiness and has a direct effect on our self-identification, self-esteem, and our mental and physical health. I don't think we can change this basic need to be recognized by the herd. All we can do is to stop being consumed by it.

I've found that that's a real danger when you've gained a bit of acknowledgment; unless you can mitigate the effects of such recognition, you run the risk of becoming dangerously self-obsessed as so many in the limelight—through social media or otherwise—tend to be.

What does all this have to do with this point in the story? The answer lies in my all-too-human tendency to have to learn the same lesson again and again—and again.

For Chantal and me, as for all human parents of a firstborn, time in those early weeks and months after Topper Tinsley's arrival moved by the second, and every second was intense, so the days, weeks, and months passed very slowly. Once passed, however, the time seemed to have sped by in a rush, a contradiction I had heard before that now, finally, made sense. It was simultaneously the best of times and the worst of times: intense pleasure and enormous stress cycled together in a beautiful blur.

Then, like all the other inevitabilities in life, Topper Tinsley began to almost sleep through the night, thus bringing about a new normalcy. Since I was getting slightly more sleep, I began checking our Instagram and email accounts again, something I had pretty much neglected since our boy's birth.

They say timing is everything in life, and in this case, it was certainly crucial, as I discovered we had been contacted again by the very nice woman who worked for the Shorty Awards. Her email, with its enthusiastic use of exclamation points, informed us that we were finalists in the category of Instagrammer of the Year and included another invite to the livestreamed awards show to be held in Times Square. She said she thought it would be "worthwhile" for us to attend.

To say this news came as a shock would take sarcasm to its ultimate edge. Shock doesn't come close. Having put every iota of our attention into Chantal's comfort and Topper Tinsley's imminent arrival, we both had entirely forgotten we were in competition for the award. All those many months of baby anticipation, preparation, and lack of sleep had drastically shifted our priorities. Once, it had been all about growing our account. Now, it was all about family. As I stared at the Shorty Awards email, with Rosenberg and Chantal both sleeping next to me on our bed and Topper Tinsley slumbering like a koala bear inches away in his bassinet, a sudden surge of excitement—the thrill of being recognized for our project—shot adrenaline through my veins. At the top of the flood, however, and just as fast, came a rush of guilt, ten times stronger than the excitement.

And so the passion for our project came and went.

Wide-awake, I looked at my peacefully sleeping family. Alone for the first time in months, an old, unhealthy habit reared its head, and I found myself once again asking questions I didn't want to know the answers to. How did I get here? Was this real or just a dream? Could someone as disturbed on the inside and so destined for dysfunction as I clearly am actually end up in this storybook situation? Was I going to wake up from this fantasy like a character in *Vanilla Sky* or *Total Recall*? My mind spun, the newer, improved version of myself giving way to my familiar self-sabotage mode until, with my right hand, I smacked myself in the face.

Everyone still slept calmly, blissfully unaware of my unhealthy internal struggle. So I gave myself an inner pep talk, beginning with the acknowledgment that I was, in fact, the luckiest person on the planet. Whether I deserved this beautiful family or not, here they were, and here I was. They were my family; nothing else mattered. I had all I needed in life. The last thing I wanted to do was go back to the ego that needed an award; this would be flying too close to the sun, falling back into my old, messed-up ways, revisiting someone I no longer wanted to be. Going to this awards show or receiving any other recognition from the outside world was definitely narcissistic, possibly unhealthy, and completely unnecessary. We would, therefore, decline the honor—both in protest against my self-absorbed tendencies and, mostly, because we already had everything we needed.

As if on cue, Chantal woke up just then. I told her about the email, my thinking, and eventual conclusion; she listened, then completely disagreed. She did not mince her words. Now, she said, more than ever, we needed to continue the mission we started. To make Topper Tinsley proud, and because we were now closer than ever, we had to stay true to our dreams. She was steadfast in insisting that, as the parents of a human, we had a greater responsibility than ever to make more people dog lovers so *their* lives could be as fulfilling as ours were. Winning an award, she maintained, could be humongous exposure for that cause. Bottom line: acting out, once again, my pseudophilosophical "ideals"—read hang-ups—would be dysfunctional, shortsighted self-sabotage and would inevitably haunt us again and again and again.

As had happened often in the past, I was masterfully put in my place. Then Chantal's mother confirmed she would watch Topper Tinsley the night of the awards show, which would be the first time we would ever not be near him, which, despite knowing this was healthy, made me incredibly uneasy.

So, nervous but now seeing the light, believing that Chantal knew what was best, and having been walked back onto the right track, I agreed: we would attend the awards show and play the game in hopes of winning the award then and there.

While it's natural to have jitters in anticipation of a huge, loud, crowded event, for those of us with a history of social phobia, the lead-up to such an event can be debilitating. This accounted for the pit in my stomach as the car dropped us off under the glaring Times Square lights in front of the venue, the PlayStation Theater. Seconds later, a person working the event recognized Rosenberg, greeted us warmly, handed us badges, then ushered us onto a faux red carpet, where we were taken aback by a blinding blitzkrieg of camera flashes. We were then directed into a colossal building and a situation that felt, thanks to the marketing people dressed mostly in suits and purposeful facial expressions, like a concert-venue-turned-business-convention. As I was already on edge—naturally—their formality made me second-guess our decision to wear colorful, donkey-themed suits and to carry matching purses, all of which symbolized our solidarity with this mistreated animal who epitomized our goal of shining a light on the underappreciated and empathizing with the underdog—a connection no one but us would get.

But as we rode up an escalator that would take us deeper into the Vegas-like labyrinth, we felt more at ease. We noticed other "internet people" who also stood out. They were dressed in casual outfits, with unconventional hairstyles, and a few even carried props and costumes. So we followed the crowd into a ballroom lined with booths sponsored by social media and technology companies. It was here that people congregated, drank, munched on hors d'oeuvres, and held on tight to the branded gift bags the booths were offering. Out of nowhere a fair-skinned bald man in a suit approached us, quickly announcing that he handled marketing for a car rental company and was a huge fan of Rosenberg and our work. Flattered, I greeted him in turn, but a wave of nausea suddenly overtook me, and I had to apologize profusely for cutting the conversation short.

The sheer number of people and the noise they made caused a rush of panic in me. To combat it, the three of us picked up speed as we moved around the pulsating crowd in search of breathing space, respite, relief. The constant motion just made me feel more panicky, until we went through a huge door and found ourselves at what appeared to be the top level of a vast concert auditorium. We peered down and saw countless tables, now just starting to fill up, all facing a huge stage with a podium shaped like a shark. That had to be where the main action would take place. The growing throngs of people and accompanying clangor brought savage twinges to my sinuses, which took every iota of self-control to suppress.

I picked up Rosenberg so he wouldn't have to walk down the stairs, and we consulted the seating chart and finally found our table, which was filled with—judging by their appearance at least—other internet personalities, many accompanied by an agent or a manager in a casual suit. We sat down, settled in, and felt we had found refuge—until I noticed that not just our table but the entire huge room was packed. At that moment, my worst nightmare—forced small talk with strangers—grabbed me by the throat. Hundreds of people were talking over one another, creating a discordant racket that sent my anxiety continuum soaring, which in turn caused my stomach to twitch, only for nausea to follow.

Blood rushed to my head, and sweat began forming all over my body and soaking into my clothes. I put Rosenberg on my lap and stroked his head, the one action that could still stop my brain from imploding. I took note of my surroundings and saw Chantal fielding fast questions from a young man in a tuxedo seated to her left. That meant I was forced to listen to the immaculately dressed, rather clean-cut thirty-something man to my right. He introduced himself as an agent and immediately began bragging about the TV shows that starred his client, a youthful but stone-faced woman in her late twenties who sat on his other side. I conjured every question about them I could possibly think of and listened intently to the answers, but I had run out my string, and the inevitability I dreaded most, a long, awkward silence, ensued.

Finally, after ten painful minutes of complete silence, the agent asked me what our talent was and why we were wearing donkey-themed outfits. Why, he wanted to know, his expression a mix of curiosity and confusion, were we here?

Flummoxed, of course, and with sweat moistening the first layer of my clothes, I started to answer, and just as the words came out, my hand somehow jerked and accidentally knocked over his glass of red wine, which landed, in a pattern recalling a monotone Jackson Pollock painting, all over his white shirt, white tie, and previously spotless light-gray suit. With the speed of a springbok, I immediately doused a napkin with my club soda and began to dab at the stains. This act, however, was stopped abruptly by the agent's gut reaction, which was to scream. "GET THE FUCK OFF ME!," effectually stealing attention away from the stage and from everyone else in the room.

To say I was mortified by both my clumsy blunder and his humiliating response would be a colossal understatement. Making the situation worse, everyone at our table remained dead silent. In fact, conversation only resumed when my "victim" insincerely apologized to me for yelling, which only increased the degradation. This had started off as a shaky evening, but spending the rest of it next to someone I had spilled a drink on and who seemingly hated me for it was well beyond shaky; it was horrendous, a complete disaster. I tried to mitigate this by turning to Chantal, but she was happily engrossed with the young guy in the tux and in what seemed to be a lively conversation. So I turned my attention to the show, which was now in full swing.

The awards seemed to cover every social media site and category one could think of, but in time, I did notice a pattern. One by one, almost everyone seated at our table was called to the stage to collect an award, as if the organizers had purposely seated all the winners together.

This seemed to mean we would win! For us that could be the best news in the history of the universe. For me specifically, however, it came with an unanticipated consequence. While I had known winning wasn't impossible, I had figured that since we were up against so many much bigger accounts, our chances were low, and as a result, I hadn't prepared a speech. I guess I figured that if we did win, I'd just wing it.

And indeed, winging it might have been possible were I not experiencing a return of all my social phobias in full swing. The thought of standing there alone and speaking before an audience of three hundred people and millions more streaming the show set my heart afire with pure panic. It beat faster and faster as I sat there, following the schedule and noting that our category, Instagrammer of the Year, was getting closer and closer to being awarded. Fight-or-flight chemicals warred within me. Panic surged. Sweat beaded my forehead, my chest, my palms, my lower back. As if this weren't enough, having drunk too much club soda, my most pressing need was for a bathroom. But Chantal forbade me from leaving the table in fear that she might have to collect the award on her own.

So my bladder was screaming, my brain was pounding, and my heart was racing, and then, in the middle of the most crowded room of my life and in the jarring mixture of speeches, music, and hundreds of people talking, suddenly, everything went still.

I sensed that a dream, the biggest accolade of my life, hovered very near, but I was imploding inside. My body tingled from head to toe, and my brain began playing tricks on me. I was fifteen again, and Angelina, the first love of my life, had just dumped me for my best friend. My parents had plucked me from public school and condemned me to private school. I was back at Enchanted, eating alone, wishing I was someone else while eavesdropping on Danny and Richie, who referred to me as Pizza Face.

Just like that moment and just like my attempts to fit in with the fraternity crowd in college and with "buddies" after college, I felt that I was still and always would be the perpetual outsider. For a second I came back to reality, only to scold myself for having a pity party at the precipice of this defining moment and for being so ungratefully pigheaded as to not appreciate the privilege. I knew this self-hatred well, but the anguish it generated swirled within me nevertheless.

Then from the podium, I heard our names called as the winners of the Instagrammer of the Year award. It was like waking up suddenly in the dead of night. I was caught off guard; I could not move. Chantal noticed, grabbed my hand, and said, "Let's go."

I stood up with Rosenberg in my arms, and we walked toward the stage together. Lightheaded, I lost my balance for a moment and almost tripped. So Chantal guided me as we walked up the stairs onto the stage.

There we were handed the award by the host, the vivaciously hilarious Keke Palmer, who hugged us, then motioned us to the podium to speak. I felt that my heart beating out of my chest must be visible to all; I seemed to be on another planet.

Chantal walked closer, kissed me on the neck, then whispered into my ear, "I love you. You guys got this."

Every cell in my body was trembling as I took a step closer to the podium. I concentrated on the feeling of Rosenberg's divine fluff in my hands, and then without stuttering, I said, "I'm Topher Brophy and am so honored to be up here right now, and honest-

ly, it's undeserved. I'm just a very average man with an extraordinary, handsome puppy and an insanely talented and beautiful wife,
the Dog Styler, Chantal Adair, who is right next to me. She is the
mastermind and the creative voice behind our account. For anyone
who has ever been called 'weird,' anyone who ever had confidence
problems, ever felt like you don't belong: you're not alone. As *Homo
sapiens*, if we act with empathy and follow our hearts, we can all do
amazing things, and this is a small example. From the bottom of our
hearts, thank you so much."

Chapter 24

A New Normal: Abnormal!

ONE OF THE MOST CONTESTED concepts in mankind's history—and certainly in my life's history—has been the definition, supposedly an objective definition, of what is considered to be normal. For me the word was always a trigger. For as far back as I can remember, it was heard in a particular context: whether I was normal or whether or not I fit in—an answer, always provided first by others then by myself, that was invariably a resounding no.

As a result, I had always associated not being "normal" with the shame, frustration, self-loathing, depression, and self-denial that plagued me. I was far from the only person who suffered in this way, and I certainly wish hindsight were twenty-twenty because it wasn't until later in life that I and so many others who were thought of as "abnormal" kids finally learned *there is no such thing as normal.* In fact, we would come to realize—and even celebrate—that the very things that make us stand out as unique turn out to be our greatest strengths. Dr. Seuss summed this up succinctly when he asked, "Why fit in when you were born to stand out?" Still, it wasn't until after years of self-hatred and repressing what made me different that I finally took the sage advice the good doctor had offered in *The Cat in the Hat*.

And I didn't exactly do it alone. I had help from Rosenberg and from Chantal, and now I even had what felt like validation from society at large. So after what seemed like a lifetime of being tortured by the very word and having arrived at a place of pretty complete contentment, I decided that, because words matter, it was time to take away the destructive power of that word by claiming new ownership of it. After all, I had two beautiful children, a wife I couldn't love more, and a profession and life's work that not only benefited others but had even been recognized as doing so in the form of a notable award. Surely, the demons were now at bay, and I was about to enter into my very own "new normal."

I knew I was an imperfect man with a history riddled with heartbreak and mistakes I didn't want to ever relive. So I asked myself what kinds of guardrails I would need to keep me in this sweet spot in which I found myself. What principles—what rules—did I need to apply to hold onto my new normalcy?

I offer them now in the hope that someone reading this may be able to relate to or may even be inspired by my list; after all, we are all cut from a similar template. So here's what I need to stay in my "new normal" and, simply, to be happy:

I need affection (who doesn't?), which for me comes in the form of at least a few close relationships with both animals and humans, and despite what dead philosophers say, I also need validation—affirmation that I am at least in some sense a worthwhile person. In fact, it is very likely that I need validation way more than most people.

I need my own personal mission or goal or higher purpose, which needs to be something that sounds crazy and unattainable, especially to me.

I need to be busy—almost constantly—working hard for something that benefits other people, fighting for the greater good, fulfilling a higher purpose. Because I don't believe there is any universal meaning in life, pursuing this work becomes a religion of sorts for me, and reaching for that higher purpose—aiming at accomplishing it—provides context for just about everything I say or do.

I always need an activity, even if it's just for its own sake. I need to be involved in the creation of things. And I've learned that all our human problems and hardships and conflicts and contradictions can serve as a muse for creating things—and that the result, as well as the creating itself, can be a form of vital therapy.

I need to keep learning. Through the thousands of people who reached out through email or social media in reaction to our work, I learned I was not alone. We are all broken, without exception, every single one of us. The thousands of people who told us about their hardships—debilitating illnesses, losing animals or humans, betrayals, disappointments, malaise, loneliness—made it clear that suffering is universal. And anyone who hides or denies this, either in real life or on social media, is a liar. I learned there is nothing that can fix all of this in all of us. But if we are lucky enough to learn as we go and eventually understand ourselves, we can find a way—our own way—to keep our center of gravity.

Finally, of all the guardrails I've built in my own life, the greatest, most important, and most powerful is: I need animal companionship.

With these essentials in place, my emotionally pain-free, double-dad life commenced. While much of it was the same, my more optimistic outlook enabled me to relish the pleasure I increasingly took in nursing and bonding with Topper Tinsley, my poignant pumpkin of a miraculously mercurial yet incessantly smiley baby boy. I also took endless pleasure in watching Topper Tinsley with Rosenberg, who was now leaping into his crib and playing tug-of-war with his toys. I was not surprised that Chantal, with her nurturing instincts and her doting love for Rosenberg, was a total natural as a human mom, and her resulting seraphic satisfaction caused her to glow with a natural high.

With everything going so well, and actually being able to sleep after taking what felt like an extended break for our nesting phase, we were ready to get back to work.

It felt good. We remembered why we loved doing it: because it ignited our creativity and was fun and, we believed, really did help to make the world a better place—by making people smile, by showing them other sides of life, by being clever and funny and real.

So we first addressed the many people who, after becoming parents of human children, treat their dogs as second-class citizens, actually discarding them in many cases, or certainly giving them less attention. We illustrated the idea in a video in which I wore a fluorescent work vest emblazoned with the words "Service Human," accompanied by the song "You Can Count on Me" by Bruno Mars. The video totally overturned the idea of a service dog as I was seen hand-feeding Rosenberg his meals, bathing him in a bubble bath, carrying him across puddles in the street, and grooming him.

The video went viral. We felt a new fervor and took it from there.

We honored our heroes, Mother Teresa, Mr. Rogers, Gandhi, and the Golden Girls.

We asked our followers to look at other sides of life as we featured the trans community, beat the drum against every form of bigotry, and noted everyday heroes like police dogs and lifeguards and navy commanders and Olympic athletes.

And sometimes our new burst of creativity just exemplified social media at its wildest. We came up with our own versions of great movies—from *The Wizard of Oz* to *Edward Scissorhands* to *Breakfast at Tiffany's*. We portrayed heavy metal singers, explained why people shouldn't harm insects, and recreated the story of Passover and the famous painting *American Gothic*—not simultaneously.

We thought it might be fun to incorporate Topper Tinsley into photos, and we also thought he would get a real kick out of it later in life. When he was in the mood, he appeared as Bamm-Bamm from

The Flintstones, as Diego Rivera next to Frida Kahlo, and as Bart from *The Simpsons*.

All of this, not to mention the Instagram award, inspired another round of interest from the press as well as from a number of reality TV show producers interested in creating a show around us. It was flattering, but to my eye, many of these shows enabled and encouraged the narcissism of their subjects. It also seemed to me that reality TV shows engineered and promoted conflicts among characters, which struck me as exploitative and in direct opposition to our own mission of trying to make the world a better place. Certainly, such shows would have widened our exposure and offered financial rewards, but we declined as gracefully as possible.

We also declined just about all the many media requests, with one exception—the Australian morning show *Sunrise*, which we had appeared on once before. This kind of show was my favorite medium—live TV—because it was a medium I could control. While the last time we appeared on *Sunrise* was in homage to our late hero Steve Irwin (RIP), on this occasion, we had more lead time, so we were able to come up with something spectacularly special.

Through the genius of a professional prosthetic makeup artist who attached real hair all over my face, said face perfectly replicated Rosenberg's, while a high-end Chewbacca costume made us a head-to-toe match. Thus attired, we were projected into the biggest morning show in Australia, and once the shock of my appearance was overcome, the interview got going.

First, of course, came the usual pleasantries from the two hosts, after which I took a sip of a milklike beverage visible in a glass marked "Rosenberg & Topper Tinsley's Father."

One of the hosts asked me what I was drinking, so I explained simply that Chantal was producing an overabundance of breast milk, and as a family that valued conservation, apart from the milk's being nutritious and delicious, we didn't let anything to go to waste.

That stunned the host, as I'd hoped. So I launched into my monologue, explaining at some length the many ways dogs and all animals make us better people and improve our lives, and claiming that as a sign of respect for dogs helping us survive as a species and for their easing of our emotional anguish in the modern world, we should all collectively give them a few moments of silence.

The speechless hosts then projected onto their screen the photo of our family in the hospital directly after Topper Tinsley's birth, the one where Rosenberg and I were both dressed as doctors. "Tell us about the experience," one of them suggested.

I spoke about what a champion Chantal was, then noted that as our firstborn, Rosenberg naturally had a role in the birth, and at the last second, I lost my nerve, requiring Rosenberg to bite off the umbilical cord with his teeth.

Despite the fact that the two hosts were both Australians and entertainers—which should have guaranteed a double sense of humor—their faces went gray with complete disbelief. Then one of them, presumably thinking the show must go on, asked, "What did the doctor say?"

My face was as straight as a pole as I explained that it was a beautiful birth and that my wife is a strong woman, so with all due respect, I would rather focus on celebrating life.

I then talked a bit about my own life, about feeling as a child that I never fit in, that I was not "normal." Animals can help us accept ourselves and one another and celebrate human eccentricities, I went on to say, as I talked about the workshops we were ideating to help people resolve conflict through animal companionship, which would involve interacting with the beauty and innocence of puppies to help those at odds see the other in a more humane and empathetic light, unconsciously increasing the odds of a resolution or reconciliation.

As the interview was about to wrap up, Rosenberg and I had one last announcement to make. So I told the world, which included our friends and our expanded digital family, our most exciting news: we had another human baby on the way!

To this day I can earnestly say that second Australian TV appearance was just about the most fun I've ever had. If this was what my "new normal" was like, I didn't want it to ever end.

Chapter 25

Tough, Tense, Twisted Turns

WE'RE A PECULIAR SPECIES, AREN'T we? Highly complicated, capricious, spontaneous, often unstable, laden with sentimental biases and continually in conflict with our instincts and our rationality. I've often wondered if it's possible for such a species to live a blissful life, which seems to be our universal goal.

At this juncture in my story, the optimist in me was experiencing that very thing—a blissful life—and therefore believed totally that goal was reachable. At the same time, the pessimist I had always been whispered in my ear that it was not, leaving the two of me to arrive at a compromise: a blissful life is possible—but for short periods of time.

The all-too-human tendency to rarely, if ever, appreciate something like contentment or happiness or joy well enough until it is gone prevents us from reveling in that bliss. And given our mortality and our margin for error, combined with everyone else's mortality and margins for error, and given that the ecosystems we inhabit contain an unquantifiable number of moving parts, there is something very close to an inevitability that, given enough time, something unpredictable and perilous will absolutely happen to us or to someone we know.

The events I'm writing about right now took place from 2018 to 2020. That was a time that, if not blissful in the global sense, now seems comparatively innocent—or certainly, very different from what came after it. For me it was a truly blissful calm before the storm that was to follow—so blissful that, as I write this in retrospect in 2021, it seems almost otherworldly.

Topper Tinsley had learned how to walk, had achieved all his childhood milestones, and was progressing as ideally as a little boy could. Despite no longer being an only child, Rosenberg had adjusted superbly, retaining his divine status within the family. He would soon be called on to adjust yet further for his new sibling. Chantal was finding this pregnancy comparatively pain-free. Our work continued to inspire us and others, and we were spending more time creating in a beach community on the far eastern end of Long Island, which offered an entirely new backdrop and motivated us to develop videos with higher production values. We were now incorporating homemade props and more sophisticated handmade set designs as we created storylines that didn't just grab attention but offered a beginning, a middle, and an end.

One such example took place on a wide, golden-sand beach to the soundtrack of the B-52s' "Rock Lobster." Rosenberg and I, dressed up in crab costumes, paraded through the streets of a small town and in and out of supermarkets—to the confusion of onlookers. Eventually, we ended up in a fish store, where we purchased multiple crabs, then unbound their claws and liberated them into the ocean.

At certain angles, the beach backdrop also passed as a desert, which allowed us to recreate Old Testament scenes while also paying respect to ancient Egypt and other civilizations of the past. Our aim was to make the educational point, as strongly as we could, of how these cultures affect us in the present and will continue to do so into the future.

We came back to Brooklyn, where our videos sought to shine a light on holidays *not* native to our cultures—Ramadan and Diwali as just two examples. The point was to show our respect for these cultures and to encourage others to do the same.

On the charity front, we coheadlined and promoted an auction event for two amazing organizations: Ubuntu Pathways, which focuses on education as a way to break the cycle of poverty in South Africa, and Operation Smile, which provides cleft palate surgery and related support that transforms the lives of children who need it most.

It wasn't all serious, though. In a slew of dance-centric videos, we paid tribute to the movie *Flashdance*, the C+C Music Factory song "Gonna Make You Sweat," and Vanilla Ice and MC Hammer. We wanted to make ourselves and others laugh, continuing to flex our never-take-life-or-ourselves-too-seriously comedic muscles.

Rosenberg and I also staged spectacles, which Chantal turned into videos, especially for Topper Tinsley. In one, we dressed as Elmo and handed out Elmo dolls to kids in Brooklyn. In another, filmed on Halloween, we wore pumpkin suits and gave small pumpkins to kids and long, painfully awkward hugs to complete strangers. We also paid homage to the genius of Liberace, dressed as Santa Claus and Hanukkah Harry (since Rosenberg identifies as Jewish), and personified Princess Meghan (me) and Prince Harry (Rosenberg).

When Chantal was about six months pregnant but still feeling great, we decided to pull off a prank for April Fools' Day, which had become a tradition for us. The year before, we had documented putting a tattoo of Rosenberg's likeness, which looked completely real, on my forehead. This time, in an attempt to outfox any of our followers who might suspect a repeat, we initiated the prank on March 1, a full month early, to convince people I had become addicted to facial piercings. To pull this off, our prosthetic experts swung into action, starting with a nose ring, which, I announced, was something I had always dreamed of and now had the confidence to pull off. But that was just the beginning of what would end up as a series of twelve different facial piercings, including a dog paw print charm that hung from a chain attached from my ear to my nose, the perfect touch. While we shot all of them in one day, we released the series gradually, *adding* piercings one by one throughout the month of March, until my whole face began to look infected with pus.

It was an elaborate ruse that went off without a hitch and inspired a lot of our followers to go wild. It was something of a high, putting our collective creativity to work in a fun, new way.

But of course it was at the top of that high, at the apex of the blissful time we were experiencing, when out of nowhere, it all came to a halt. Topper Tinsley came down with a fever. In retrospect, that is when everything changed. The downward spiral that followed reminded me of a T-shirt I had once seen: a photo of Axl Rose in his prime that read, "Nothing lasts forever."

It started out benignly enough—as a normal toddler cold or flu. Just a light fever, no real cause for alarm, until he suddenly took a turn for the worse. The fever spiked and kept spiking, climbing all the way to 105 degrees, high enough to cause him to shiver uncontrollably and for the doctor to tell us to immediately submerge him in an ice bath. Once the fever went down, we took him to the hospital, where it was confirmed there was no fluid in his lungs—thus ruling out pneumonia and suggesting just close monitoring and lots of bed rest.

At the same time, late in 2019, we had begun hearing and reading about a new coronavirus that had spread in China; as it was nowhere near coming to the United States, it didn't seem a concern. Then, as I was constantly with T, I seemed to catch a bit of what he had in the form of a pretty awful sore throat and head cold. Again, we didn't think this meant anything at the time—it was a sore throat and head cold!—but as Chantal was almost seven months pregnant, Topper Tinsley and I both stayed as far away from her as possible.

Since both of us were now sick, we watched the news a lot and began to hear talk about the spread of the new coronavirus, now dubbed COVID-19. Still, there wasn't a single confirmed case of it in the United States.

Until suddenly there was. Out of nowhere and seemingly all at once, every news source in every medium was headlining the spread of this mysterious virus. While there was as yet no way to test for the disease, a sudden influx of sick people flooding hospitals raised suspicion that the virus had reached New York.

Our family buckled down. Topper Tinsley and I stayed on the couch, and Chantal and I began to worry. One night she felt extra tired and sick, but it passed, and she again felt fine. Topper Tinsley's fever, which had been raging for a week, finally went down, but my bad cold was still in full swing.

Then came the first reports that hospitals in New York City were becoming overrun with what they thought were COVID-19 patients. At this point, there was mass confusion and no sure knowledge as to whether the virus was airborne or not. No one knew for certain how it was spread, but what *was* clear was that it was spreading rapidly and that hospitals were not safe. This was, of course, frightening for everyone, but with Chantal seven months pregnant and a toddler and me showing symptoms that could have been COVID-19, we were a particularly intense, particularly stressful mess.

Like millions of others, we were glued to the news, social media, and the endless chatter, all of it conveying an ever-worsening situation. Supplies—medicine, bottled water, diapers, canned food—

were out of stock both online and everywhere in our neighborhood, turning our stress into outright panic. It felt surreal, like a bad apocalypse movie. The news only grew bleaker, supplies continued to dwindle, hospitals in the city were so overcrowded that auxiliary institutions had to be pressed into service.

With the upcoming birth looming, and with Topper Tinsley and me both now feeling better but still symptomatic, it seemed clear that all of us should be someplace safer and that none of us should be around other people. Chantal and I were pretty certain we needed to make a key decision: whether to leave the city and go someplace less populated, and if so, where and when.

We began to scour Airbnb for available houses in the Catskills, where we had gotten married, but adding to all our other woes, it seemed everyone else had the same idea. There were few choices left—places that looked uninhabitable, lacked an internet connection, and most importantly, didn't allow dogs, which we thought was discriminatory and should have been a punishable crime in itself. In desperation I had barely known until then, I messaged every house I could, pleading our case and asking if they would allow our dog, even sending his social media account and philanthropic credentials. Finally, a person with a house near the town of Tannersville, New York, nearly three hours by car from Brooklyn, accepted my plea, and we were booked for the next day.

Relieved, we started packing like crazy, loading everything we thought we'd need into our luggage, including all the cold and flu medicine we could get our hands on. In a mad dash, and at this point, panic having deprived us of any real sleep for days, we packed virtually everything we owned into our SUV, just barely closing its doors, and on March 15, at midnight, we left our Brooklyn apartment and were on our way.

It was a memorable drive, vivid and intense. It was a cold night, and halfway to our destination, Topper Tinsley vomited. This was a common occurrence for him, but the problem this time was that we didn't have a change of clothes handy, and out of fear of catching the virus or giving it to someone else by stopping somewhere, we had to make do by using my shirt to wipe off the vomit and other clothes of mine to wrap him up again.

By the time we had left the highway and were following directions to the house, our cell service and GPS had lost reception, and we were lost. As if that weren't enough, as we were consistently gaining elevation, it suddenly started to snow, hard, leaving us with zero visibility. Soon after, with Topper Tinsley awake and vomiting again, with snow pelting down, with me already doing all I could to hold it together, I heard a police siren and, through the downpour, made out the cop cruiser coming up behind me, signaling us to pull over. I apologized about a burned-out taillight and begged for directions from the helpful cop, and we were again on our way.

It took many more wrong turns, but at long last, we arrived at our Airbnb. We were exhausted and petrified, suspecting we had entered an alternate reality or some other hellish dimension. My wife, with her humongous baby bump, was awake, and Topper Tinsley was now sleeping but continued to smell of vomit, an odor that seemed to have penetrated all the way into the fissures of his safety seat.

I think we were all nevertheless glad and grateful to have arrived at our temporary new home, until we discovered that the keys were not where they should have been and that the door was, of course, locked.

Repeatedly, we called the owner and his manager—to no avail. It was 3:00 a.m. We were gasping in sheer disbelief at our predicament and marveling at the unlikelihood of this many things going this wrong. The car was quickly becoming covered in snow, and we had no other options. So we gave up. Chantal and I looked at each other and just laughed. At least, we figured—and hoped—this was the most precarious position we would ever find ourselves in.

Flummoxed, with no other ideas and virtually no alternative, on a whim, we phoned the hotel that had hosted our wedding, the Emerson Resort. Unlike just about all other hotels in the region, it had not yet closed down and had a room available—ironically, the very room we had stayed in for our wedding. We took it as an indication that our luck might have taken a turn.

Whether that potential change of luck was pure happenstance or some form of divinely orchestrated coincidence didn't matter. The notion that after the most harrowing car ride of our lives, we could enjoy the desperately needed creature comforts of this hotel suite of such happy memories exemplified for us the mindset we would need for the immediate future—and likely for the rest of our lives: bliss can only be temporary, so never sweat the small stuff, enjoy the little things, don't take anything or anyone for granted, and be grateful for what you have because things can—and very likely will—get worse.

Chapter 26

Storm-Born

I'M SURE YOU CAN RECALL in detail where you were, what you were doing, and how it felt when COVID-19 was officially declared a pandemic. It was a moment when the world unambiguously lost every iota of its innocence. For us that moment took place the very next morning after the events of the last chapter. That's when New York State shut down the Emerson Resort and we were finally let in to our cramped, creepy, but seemingly COVID-free Airbnb near the top of a mountain.

After we unpacked and all settled into the same musty room, Topper Tinsley let loose a flurry of terrible-two tantrums, par for the course, which in this case came from a combination of disorientation and boredom. In between efforts to calm him down by singing songs and reading books to him, we were glued to the news, which was cataclysmic.

The number of cases rose and rose. Schools and businesses shut down. Authority figures could not agree on a course of action. We, like everyone else, were isolated, helpless, rudderless, hysterical, and panicked, hoping it was all a harrowingly realistic dream. All we could do, quarantined inside as day after day passed, was to call everyone we knew to send love and see if they were infected, and as someone inevitably knew someone who had it, we just watched the pandemonium skyrocket. Without any concrete information on how the virus was spread, everyone was a potential enemy. It was the survival of the most paranoid stranger against stranger, it brought out the *Lord of the Flies* in everyone.

As a city slicker in colorful, patterned clothes, I stuck out like a sore thumb in the country supermarket. I was yelled at and even spat on by locals who sensed I was from "the city" and cursed me for taking their food and spreading the virus.

This also played out at the town dump, where the heavyset man with a gray beard and clad in full camo who collected the money, screamed, "GET BACK!" while pushing me with a pot attached to a broomstick—a dual-purpose makeshift instrument that allowed him to collect money *and* maintain social distancing. Because City People are, of course, the ones known for turning their noses up at Country People, the irony made me laugh. If I put myself in their shoes, I could empathize with their anger and could understand how privileged we were to have a car and the financial means to leave the city—even though, as a native New Yorker, leaving a place that felt intertwined with my soul was gut-wrenching. With a wife almost ready to give birth, a toddler who put everything in his mouth, and a fur son who constantly needed to go outside for walks, I knew leaving the city was the safest course of action. But it also came at a humongous cost: we now had no idea where or by whom our baby would be delivered. New York City hospitals were clearly overrun, and spouses were barred from being in delivery rooms, so for us, going back wasn't an option.

I spent an entire day, with Topper Tinsley screaming in the next room and Chantal trying to console him, calling every ob-gyn within a twenty-mile radius from our temporary home. To my utter disbelief, because we came from the place that was now the epicenter of the COVID outbreak, every single doctor refused us. I was beginning to think I would be forced to deliver the baby myself, and this created an entirely new level of panic that literally made my hands shake.

I considered finding another Airbnb in another state, but *everything* that looked halfway decent was booked or had an explicit no-dog rule. Moreover, there were rumors that the federal government might begin banning interstate travel. Making the situation exponentially worse, our Airbnb owner messaged us, apologized for ending our stay so that his family could use the house and, as it turned out, was legally able to break the contract thanks to a small-print clause. When I protested, my voice oscillating between being on the verge of tears and rage, he asked me to put myself in his shoes and consider whether I would not do everything I could to protect my own family. He had me; I couldn't argue the point.

With no ob-gyn, a new baby's imminent arrival, and now no place to live, I finally went over the edge. Chantal and Topper

Tinsley were in the next room, so I made no noise. I just sat on the yellow-and-red-striped linoleum floor of the bathroom of this 1960s-era house, shaking, my mind attacking itself, my stomach in knots, sweat pouring all over me. Just then Topper let loose with another tantrum, broke what I later learned was a lamp in the house, and began wailing like a siren.

I often told myself things could always be worse, but this was a new low, and I wasn't sure how. All my rules about staying functional and happy, everything I had learned all went out the window. I couldn't think of any way to solve these problems, and I found myself pacing back and forth, a walking catastrophe.

At some point in the midst of this pacing, my eyes steadfastly staring at the hideous and—quite likely—asbestos-laden floor, I noticed Rosenberg, who had been assiduously guarding Chantal and Topper Tinsley, now began following me. Back and forth, he paced just behind me. I looked down at him, and it seemed to me that despite the unmitigated chaos, his enchanting, honey-green eyes that coordinated perfectly with his many shades of brown fur, seemed unfazed, even happy.

It made sense. Of course he was happy. All he cared about was being with his family, and here we all were. Everything else—the continually catastrophic news, leaving behind our home with all its creature comforts, the gargantuan anxiety about where we'd live and who would deliver the baby—was just noise to him. He was in the present and with the only people who mattered to him.

So I stopped pacing and started playing with him. I watched him scurry up and down the claustrophobic stairway and saw how much he loved his new environment. Then we went outside, and Rosenberg chased chipmunks and smelled every tree in the backyard. Back inside the house, we both plopped down on the mothball-smelling couch, where I petted him while staring at his eyes, which were open just a slit, his way of showing he was experiencing the epitome of contentment. This did not calm my terror, but his presentness, his sheer beauty in this moment of derangement, helped slow down my flailing, fractured thoughts.

I closed my eyes and reminded myself how much Rosenberg had helped me before, which ignited a little mental clarity. I had already lived through my own versions of hell, so although the world was crumbling before our eyes, I had what actually constituted the unique advantage of having prepared myself through practice. I knew it was possible to come out on the other side of emotional turmoil because I had done it. I had conquered the darkest demons. And although this moment was completely different and the stakes were a thousand times higher, I was actually prepared for this. And with Chantal in the final phase of her pregnancy, it was my responsibility to step up. It was up to me to safeguard the future of our family.

That night for the first time in weeks, I got a few hours of REM sleep, and when I awoke, it was time for war.

I called back every ob-gyn I had phoned before, but this time I used a different voice, higher pitched, with a slight Southern accent, so they wouldn't recognize me. I also pleaded a slightly different case. And I admit I told a white lie. I said we had left New York City a full month before, when the truth was half of that. It worked. A bighearted ob-gyn affiliated with Kingston Hospital, about thirty minutes away, agreed to take us in.

I called up our Airbnb host and offered to pay him off the books and double the agreed-upon fee if we could stay the full three months; that would give us time to get a little settled with the new baby, and it would afford him an alternative plan for his family. He agreed, and despite how morally ambiguous this was, I stopped to ponder both how lucky and privileged I was that I could afford it. Just like that, in a successive one-two swoop, our two biggest problems were solved.

We were happy, and for almost an hour, we forgot we were in the middle of the worst pandemic anyone alive had ever seen. Even with the news as dismal as ever and even though winter was now in full swing, the heaviest weights had been lifted, and keeping in mind the motto that things can always be worse, life didn't feel so grim. In fact, with a little bit of optimism, the family as a whole found a rhythm to our isolated life in the country and reached a new "new normal." So with our affairs relatively settled, I went back to doing what always made me happy—helping people. I went back to work.

Gone, however, were the elaborate costumes, the props, benevolent pranks, and conceptually storied videos. With Chantal ready to pop and on bed rest, I operated the camera and offered fireside chats—styled after President Franklin Roosevelt's—about feats of human ingenuity, the unlimited power of science, and even the silver linings of the pandemic.

What were those silver linings? It had dawned on me that even though many of us were separated from our parents and other loved ones, we now spoke to them on the phone and via video chats more frequently than ever before. And now that work was not taking up the majority of our time, we could finally reprioritize the most important people in our lives, our kids; we might even stop bickering over small things. Surely, this would all help strengthen our family bonds. I also noted how the shutdown of the economy might serve as a hopeful strategy to reverse the effects of climate change. Setting new priorities meant we could now filter out the noise and turn this crisis into an opportunity by enacting the change we always wanted to see in ourselves and in the world.

Of course, comedic antics were routinely mixed in with these chats. In one I confessed that Chantal was upset with me for leaving the toilet seat up and declared that all men should either try wearing diapers or pee sitting down, and yes, we donned ghillie suits while swinging sticks to the *Conan the Barbarian* theme song.

As the days went on, we went on hikes in the hills, cooked beans a thousand ways, baked banana bread, and found inventive ideas to keep Topper Tinsley and ourselves as busy as humanly possible— until one day, at 5:00 a.m. a month before the due date, Chantal's water broke, and our second *Homo sapiens* birth began.

The second we realized what had happened, we acted fast. Luckily, we had befriended an amazing woman and dog mom down the road, who dropped everything to come over and stay with Topper Tinsley and Rosenberg. Our debt to her is boundless in size and infinite in time. We drove, way over the speed limit, to Kingston Hospital, which had prison-strict COVID protocols but—unlike New York City—allowed spouses in the room, and Chantal's labor began.

Mystifyingly, minutes after the IV had been inserted into her arm, the head nurse entered the room and gave us some shocking news. Since labor was a month early, there was a decent chance the baby would need to be admitted into the newborn intensive care unit, which, as a regional hospital, Kingston did not have. If the NICU was deemed necessary, the baby would need to be airlifted by helicopter to Albany Medical Center, and by law, we could not be with our newborn in the copter.

We were in a horrible predicament. We could leave to chance that we might be separated from our baby—if the NICU was needed—or we could pack up immediately, unmount Chantal from the medical machinery, and pray she didn't give birth on the way to Albany Med an hour away.

I insisted on the latter; Chantal, already in intense labor, with her nesting instincts in full swing, did not want to risk having the baby in an ambulance and refused to leave. But I didn't give up, and after much pleading and some back-and-forth yelling, she agreed. They packed her up from her hospital bed into the ambulance, and I hopped into our car and started driving.

The one thing no one had mentioned while we were in the hospital making our decision was that a torrential thunderstorm was underway. The rain was coming down in ropes, and with almost zero visibility, every second of the drive felt like an hour. Feeling the weight of multiple lives on me, propelled by adrenaline, and racing against time made me feel like I was outside my own body in a way that was simultaneously awe-inspiring and empowering. And before I knew it, I had beaten the ambulance to our destination.

Despite the terror-stricken start and the even-higher-level prisonlike COVID security protocols at Albany Med, everything went superlatively smoothly from that moment on, and our daughter, Tippie Teddington, six pounds, two ounces, was duly born into this world, late at night, in a torrential rainstorm.

An all-women NICU team burst onto the scene the moment she arrived, clad in purple scrubs and face masks that distinguished them from the other medical personnel, who wore the standard light-blue color. The sea of people parted for the NICU team as they moved in unison, like Special Forces superheroes, examining Tippie Teddington, conducting a thoroughly detailed analysis of her lungs, then pronouncing said lungs as having passed their inspection before they left as stealthily as they came in.

Our second human baby, if I may brag again (please excuse me), like her two brothers, was a magnificent creation who received countless compliments from almost every member of the heroic medical staff who entered our room. As Chantal and I took turns holding our tiny human, who was wrapped like a tortilla in the standard blue-and-white blanket, I noticed my heart beat slow as my adrenaline and cortisol levels began to normalize. As Tippie Teddington, exhausted from the ordeal, began to sleep, Chantal closed her eyes, and so did I.

But instead of sleeping, a wave of vivid introspective thoughts began to flow in. I marveled at how lucky I was to have this beautiful, healthy baby and the irony of how she'd never truly understand the bedlam of unprecedented circumstances surrounding her entry into the world. As I sat and stared at the two of them sleeping, I thought about my other two kids waiting in our Airbnb and how grateful I was for them and how much my circumstances had changed. Here I was, in a hospital in upstate New York, in what I didn't realize then was the worst pandemic in a hundred years, and it was the happiest I'd ever been. Life was bizarre, but it was also beautiful.

Chapter 27

Animal Instinct, Human Reason

A THROUGH LINE OF THIS BOOK, one we often so perplexingly ignore, is the ongoing conflict between our animal instinct and our human reason. At this point in my story, perhaps the most appropriate way to look at this conflict is through what happens to us as new parents. We act on instinct—our very own animal instinct, temporarily drowning out our rationality, because as with all animals, the only thing that matters to us is the survival of our sublime offspring. And for those of you who have experienced this instinct from the driver's seat, from which vantage it plows over any conflict with reason, you know the emotional effect is nothing short of beautiful in a most wondrous way.

Along with the clearheaded bliss I was feeling in new parenthood, the wisdom of Rosenberg, and the trials and various errors of life, I had learned to assuage the once-constant conflicts of my brain and let my instincts guide me. Not breaking during the treacherous but, in the end, flawlessly safe birth for both Tippie Teddington and Chantal felt to me like I had passed the final and graduated. From here on out, now that I had cracked the code, life would be peachy.

Or so I thought. In the midst of a global pandemic, with a larger family and many more complex moving parts, the consequences of relying solely on gut-powered decisions—that is, decisions guided solely by animal instinct—would prove that everything I believed I had just learned was completely wrong.

Once Chantal and our daughter were discharged from the hospital, we all returned to our cramped, musty, overpriced Airbnb in the highest spirits imaginable. As Tippie Teddington had been born a full month early, she was on the small side, but fortunately, she had the appetite of a miniature horse. Rosenberg, always the family man, took to Tippie Teddington instantly, guarding and occasionally stealing licks, but Topper Tinsley was a different story. Despite preorchestrating gifts, which we told him came from Tippie Teddington, our boy was so accustomed to being the center of human attention that he reacted to his change in status with an exponentially increasing number of protest tantrums. So we had to match his emotional extortion with additional gifts from the Marvel Universe, and as he associated the gifts with his new sister, this stratagem eventually met with success.

Now, as a happy family, and despite not having time to shower, not being able to see friends or extended family, and having to wash our fruit and vegetables with soap, we spent every waking second entertaining all three kids outside with no one else around, an activity that enabled us to gain a new equilibrium. We were not scared about the next calamity that would surely come our way, as Chantal and I told each other, because we knew we had the ability to adapt.

The day after voicing this curse-in-reverse, the weather turned. It rained every day for a month straight, essentially locking us two adults, two small humans, and a very active fur child indoors in a small, uncomfortable house. And time began to move more slowly than it ever had before. We pivoted, though, reading books, playing board games, taking bath-bomb-filled showers, baking bread, squeezing orange juice by hand, and making elaborate sculptures with popsicle sticks and cardboard, passing the time in any and every way we could think of. Then, as always happens when one waits and has patience, the weather turned again.

With clear days and warmer temperatures, Rosenberg, by now bottled up with angst and cabin fever, and I, almost equally perturbed, restarted our exercise regimen. With the kids napping in the stroller, we took long walks each morning, afternoon, and evening, enjoying the beauty of the Catskill Mountains, which to this day rivals the beauty of any landscape I have ever seen. To achieve the heightened heart rates we both needed, Rosenberg and I added to this daily regimen one long tennis ball fetch session in the backyard, which was unfenced but bordered on all sides with lush, untouched woods. Because as a pup Rosenberg had demonstrated an attachment disorder—he always needed to be close to me—in the right settings, we were comfortable with him being off leash.

One afternoon, as had happened countless times before, while chasing the ball at full speed, Rosenberg caught the scent or sensed the movement of another animal and took off. I screamed his name at the top of my lungs and ran after him into the woods as fast as I could, but it was as if he had completely vanished.

I stood there, my lungs ballooning unnaturally in my chest, in complete and utter disbelief. Everything turned in slow motion as I spun in circles, trying to get a 360-degree view of the woods, but I saw nothing and heard no sounds or movement, except an eerie wind blowing through the trees. I realized my heart was pounding, each beat reverberating through my entire body, which I somehow tasted in my throat. At the same time, I felt the sweat gather at my lower back, trickle down my armpits, dampen my palms. Did my canine son's instincts, which had helped me in immeasurable ways, and which I regarded as nearly sacred, lead him astray? My brain raced with panic and confusion as I ran again, at top speed, zigzagging in every direction, covering as much ground as I could, while screaming Rosenberg's name, my voice cracking in desperation. Time stopped, and in what was the cruelest, most deranged torture, my brain churned out images of him frightened, hungry, chased by coyotes, unable to fend for himself, in desperate need of food and water. I suddenly snapped out of it, worried I might have ventured too far; maybe he had already come back and was close to home.

I ran into the house to get Chantal, who was feeding Tippie Teddington but jumped up the instant she saw my face. With Tippie Teddington still latched to her mother, we ran outside, both of us yelling for Rosenberg. Tears gushed from my eyes, and as I wiped them, I looked down at my feet and saw that my flip-flops were gone and blood was oozing from my feet from running barefoot through the woods. When I looked back up from my bloodied feet, I saw none other than Rosenberg trotting toward us, half his body wet, with a big smile on his face and a tennis ball in his mouth. I scooped him up and hugged him so tight he grunted. Still, I wouldn't let go, the worst terror I had ever felt evaporating in an instant.

Yes, a catastrophe was averted, but it changed me. The brief loss of Rosenberg was a visceral reminder that we are all one minute away from a life-shattering catastrophe that could leave us so emotionally or physically broken that living could feel worse than death.

As a direct course of action, Rosenberg would not be allowed outside without his new fifty-foot leash, and we would immediately begin the search for our permanent home, one with a fenced-in backyard.

With New York City's COVID and crime numbers continuing to climb, Chantal and I determined that setting our sights on renting a house in the Connecticut suburbs, where there were fewer wild animals and which had better access to the city, would be a safe bet. As we soon found out, though, millions of other people had the same idea to flee the pandemic, so finding a home was going to be anything but easy. It wasn't even possible to see properties in person, so when we learned about a house with a fenced-in yard, our broker put in an application sight unseen; she was told we were competing with thirty-six other families. A gut instinct prompted me to insist she include a photo of Rosenberg with the application, and because the owner was a dog fanatic, it worked! Once again, my son, my hero, my teacher and best friend, whom I had almost lost forever due to his own gut instinct, had saved the family as well as the day. And just like that, we were in the suburbs.

The house, as our changing luck would have it, was right across from a beautiful, humongous, and perpetually uncrowded park, the perfect place to be outdoors during a pandemic. Unpacking was stupendously slower and more complicated with small kids around, but like everything else, it got done, and as we had done many times, we proved our adaptability, settled into our new neighborhood, and reminded ourselves how lucky we were to have a home.

With the pandemic showing no signs of abating, and with little chance of obtaining help or getting involved in social activities, Chantal and I worked around the clock to keep the kids educated, engaged, exercised, healthy, and happy. But we were spread extraordinarily thin between starting to homeschool Topper Tinsley and ceding to Tippie Teddington's demands for undivided attention, and I noticed Rosenberg's needs were falling through the cracks. I had pledged such a thing would never happen, and this was the very first time it had. His friends were far away in Brooklyn, and COVID had deemed dog parks unsafe. So we followed our gut and accepted that the only way to cure his apathy, which we couldn't bear to witness any longer, was to get another pup—to give Rosenberg a friend.

ANIMAL INSTINCT, HUMAN REASON

A perk of having a social media network of dog parents is that just a couple days after telling people in our digital family we were looking for a puppy, we were contacted by a breeder who told us about a family who had parted ways with a recently adopted Aussiedoodle puppy with a tiny, fluffy, perplexed, guinea-pig-like face. Without asking questions, we jumped for joy and said yes.

One week later she arrived in a doggie transport van, and our entire family went out to receive her. My heart sped up substantially, and I felt goosebumps on my skin as I walked to the van, compared and confirmed the pup with her photo, and took all seven pounds of her velvet fluff into my arms. She showed not one iota of anxiety and simply began licking my face and widening her eyes as she soaked up her new environment. I took in her delightful puppy smell and thought how she had not a care or any notion that she and I lived in a pandemic-laden, cruel, cold world. At that moment, Chantal, with Rosenberg on a leash, Tippie Teddington on her hip, and Topper Tinsley at her side, suggested we name her Heaven on Earth, abbreviated to HOE. And we did.

Chantal let Rosenberg and Heaven smell each other for a few moments before we brought everyone back into the house, Rosenberg entering first. Then, to our utter shock and total dismay, the second Heaven followed him inside, Rosenberg unleashed a guttural, monstrous growl, the likes of which we had never heard from him before, just before he lunged with lightning speed to bite her.

I felt electrocuted, then frozen with shock. We had put so much thought into his need for a companion and had assumed that since she was of the opposite sex, there was no way they would not bond. But as the next few days, weeks, and indeed months would make clear, gut instincts can be catastrophically misinformed.

We made efforts to reintroduce them at a safe distance and were met with the same outcome. Rosenberg seemed possessed by a demonic bloodlust against this helpless baby puppy, and the grotesque noises he emitted when he lunged at her horrified our human kids as well as Chantal and me. Worse, when the kids started crying, we naturally raced to comfort them, and that split second was enough for Rosenberg to lunge at Heaven again. I thrust my body between our two pups as the human kids wailed even louder. Locking eyes with Chantal, I saw in her expression the same terror I was feeling, which thundered what neither of us had to articulate—"We are f***ed! What have we gotten ourselves into?"

We sought advice from a network of experts, who suggested the strategy of keeping the two dogs apart, then reintroducing them to each other slowly. We followed their methodology: tight leads on group walks, mutual treat sessions, and supervising both dogs like vultures every single second. We did this and numerous other bonding exercises repeatedly and faithfully, yet the second we let our guard down, which, while caring for the two small human kids, proved impossible to avoid, Rosenberg morphed into his satanic alter ego, occasionally even biting Heaven, which initiated a cacophony of guttural growls and squeals and poor little Heaven's pee releasing onto the floor. This gutted us more than words could express.

When our desperation neared panic, we enlisted the help of a behavioral "dog guru." His recommended philosophy was to strip Rosenberg of what he believed, mistakenly, was his alpha status. To achieve this, we were to make sure he was always last through every door and into every room, did not sit or sleep on any surface other than the floor, wore a muzzle when anywhere near Heaven, was never allowed to lick anyone in the face, and was never ever the center of attention.

Maybe this plan would have worked, but we knew it would also break his spirit, so it was a nonstarter.

The tactic we instead decided on was quite possibly just a Band-Aid or a show of procrastination, but it was the only thing we could stomach. Through the use of child gates, we simply made sure to keep the two dogs separated—relegated to different rooms on different floors at all times. A quarantine within a quarantine. We accepted our fate even while understanding that being doomed to this compartmentalized life in which we were never able to all be together would inevitably take a toll on our happiness and functionality as a family unit. There seemed no other way to solve the problem.

It's hard to overstate how difficult this situation was for Chantal and me. It all unfolded just as winter was setting in, and while the logistical challenges of keeping two dogs apart while caring for an infant and a toddler were stressful in the extreme, the emotional guilt we suffered by creating this situation was by far the harder part. We had successfully fled the city when it had become the epicenter of the pandemic, had a second baby after switching hospitals midlabor, and had—impossibly—found the perfect home. We had it all. Until we followed our gut and abandoned reason, and we now found ourselves stuck in a dysfunctional purgatory of disharmony.

For the first time in his life, Rosenberg was filled with anger, frustration, and pain; he was in as bad of shape as I had been when he came into my life. He was utterly miserable. At the same time, Heaven, the epitome of a happy, innocent soul, found herself, in the most important puppy imprint stage of her young life, abused, attacked, and intimidated. She lived in constant fear.

And then there was me, the man who had reveled in being known in some circles as the poster boy for the model Dog Dad. In my own eyes, though, I was the worst dog parent imaginable.

The feelings this ignited were not unfamiliar. I was back where I had started, the president of my own pity party, turning my anger inward. But with one colossal difference. Dark as things were, I had four kids who depended on me. Everyone had to eat, be entertained, exercise, sleep, and learn. That was all that mattered. After putting the kids to bed and cleaning the kitchen every night, I was too exhausted to wallow, obsess, or often even think about anything else, so life trucked on.

As always, we adapted, and while Rosenberg and Heaven could never be in the same room, we focused on other things, and throughout that entire winter, we managed to find our fun. When the weather started to warm up, we experimented again, walking the two pups together and holding our breath when Rosenberg did not go after Heaven right away. When we tried it again, however, it failed. But when we tried it yet a third time, Rosenberg, for the first time, stopped to sniff Heaven's butt. It had worked! Or did it? Every day saw two steps forward then one step back, but this was the best we could hope for.

Then it happened. An entire day of three joint walks without a single incident. It happened again the next day. Then the dogs were able to be in the same room, though keeping a distance. Then finally, Rosenberg ran to Heaven, and she understood to flop onto her back and submit. He accepted this, smelling her lady parts and seemingly teaching her the rules.

In time an entire year had passed, and suddenly, they were sitting next to each other, and sitting next to each other again. In what I chalk up to being one of the biggest miracles I have ever witnessed with my own eyes, today, despite the occasional kerfuffle, they are friends, and even the best of friends have kerfuffles.

Our family practiced patience, repetition, and perseverance for an entire year, but hope was our chief emotion. That our two pup children hated each other ripped my heart out every single day. As every parent knows, seeing your kids hurt each other is a special type of pain—a type I never want to experience again. Still, I learned again that if we hold on, power through despite the pain, and never lose hope, with enough effort and time, pretty much anything can be achieved. And those gut instincts that for a year I suspected of being wrong turned out to be, of course, right in the end.

So can our gut instincts ever really lead us astray? And did Rosenberg's instincts in the woods lead him astray?

Yes, I believe instincts can lead both our species astray. But it is human rationality, despite its tendency to gridlock us, that can temper any misdirection those instincts might generate. And that rationality works best of all when we have a profound understanding of ourselves, as I now do in my Rosenberg days.

He has given me so much; he has given me my life—the chance to live in Technicolor and to become who I dreamed I could be but never thought I would. He taught me how to care for another being, which is the greatest gift life affords and is, for me, the true definition of maturity—a maturity I lacked for so long. In return, I wanted to give him a canine companion who might be to him what he had been to me. That instinct appeared to be a disaster. But human rationality, as it turns out, grows up with us. Yes, that particular instinct of mine backfired big-time at first, but it also taught me to never give up. Because things will change, and the most important thing for a family to do is to stay together and power through it.

That mix of instinct and rational thought has given all six of us—Chantal, Topper Tinsley, Tippie Teddington, Rosenberg, Heaven, and me—a loving family, but it also gives us an obligation to other species in our world. Despite being able to develop languages, build societies, and achieve incomprehensible feats such as democracy, vaccines, and interstellar travel, humankind has failed miserably in how inhumanely we treat the majority of our animals. We think animals, and nature for that matter, exist for our use alone.

While the sanctity and well-being of all sentient beings should be respected, I believe dogs, specifically, deserve a sacred status and preferential treatment. From an evolutionary perspective, dogs have been pivotal to our survival through acting as our hunting partners, alarm systems, and transportation. While we no longer rely on dogs for survival, as my story and the massive increase in adoptions during the pandemic illustrate, our dependence on them remains the same. In a world where our leaders prey on our fears and exploit our differences, our species' near-universal love for dogs has tremendous potential to be utilized as a great unifier. And with exponentially more discord, disharmony, and destructive forces arising every passing day, a great unifier such as this is needed now more than ever. And as we continue to excel in scientific and technological fields, the companionship of dogs, an anchor to our evolutionary past, can safeguard our humanity.

Because being human is to suffer, my journey is in no way unique, but I do consider myself to be unimaginably lucky. Through the kismet of finding an unconditional furry love battery, I was able to crawl out of a living hell and find happiness and fulfillment. This journey has allowed me to form poignant connections with hundreds of thousands of people of all races, backgrounds, political affiliations, religions, and creeds, all because of our mutual love for animals. My digital family is proof of the power and potential dogs and other animals have to bring people together.

As a now-eternal optimist, I believe that as time passes and our species continues to evolve, our reverence for and comprehension of animals'—specifically dogs'—power to heal will continue to grow as well. As an imperfectly mortal man, there will always be much

I'll never know, but I am certain that under the right circumstances, the life of every human can be improved through the companion-ship and unconditional love of an animal child.

While adversity, pain, loss, and hardship are inevitable, our furry love batteries will charge our depleted generators with innocence, loyalty, compassion, and kindness, and with them at our sides, we'll always have hope and strive to be the best possible versions of our-selves we can be.